Treating Memory Impairments

A Memory Book and Other Strategies

•

Vicki S. Dohrmann, M.A., CCC-SLP

Communication Skill Builders ®
a division of
The Psychological Corporation
3830 E. Bellevue / P.O. Box 42050
Tucson, Arizona 85733
1-800-763-2306

Reproducing Pages from This Book

As described below, some of the pages in this book may be reproduced for instructional or administrative use (not for resale). To protect your book, make a photocopy of each reproducible page. Then use that copy as a master for photocopying.

The Learning Curve Design is a registered trademark of The Psychological Corporation.

For information about our audio and/or video products, write to us: Communication Skill Builders, a division of The Psychological Corporation, P.O. Box 42050, Tucson, AZ 85733.

Acknowledgments

I wish to extend my appreciation to B. J. Maule, Judy Rush, Donna Cole, Teresa Quinlan, Robert Richmond, the rehabilitation team at Community Home Health Care, and all my clients for offering suggestions, giving support, and using the memory strategies presented in this book.

About the Author

Vicki S. Dohrmann is in private practice as the administrator of Speech and Rehabilitation Services. In addition to assisting therapists in establishing rehabilitation programs, she develops workshops on cognitive disorders for physicians, nurses, occupational therapists, physical therapists, social workers, and other medical personnel. As part of an interdisciplinary team, she has provided diagnostic and treatment services to adolescent and adult clients with head injuries.

Ms. Dohrmann received a B.S. degree in speech-language pathology from Oregon State University, and an M.A. degree in speech-language pathology from Western Washington University. She holds the Certificate of Clinical Competence from the American Speech-Language-Hearing Association.

Contents

Introduction

Adolescents and adults experiencing memory impairments secondary to a variety of medical disorders most often experience difficulty with functional daily activities at home, school, and work. To help clients learn to deal with their impairments, clinicians have had to spend a great deal of time locating or creating materials for therapeutic use with these individuals.

Treating Memory Impairments was developed to provide clinicians with materials for assisting patients to compensate for their deficits. The book incorporates external and internal memory strategies that have proven to be effective with individuals who have memory impairments. Reproducible memory book pages are included in Chapter Nine to create individualized memory book systems. Additionally, structured tasks and reproducible worksheets are provided to help clients learn to use their memory book systems effectively.

It is important that a systematic, step-by-step training procedure be developed for each individual based on the person's skill level and needs. You will need to generate a written training program that outlines specific goals, objectives, rationale for the program, training procedures and cues, and data collection format. All individuals involved in the patient's care should be aware of the training program and procedures. Encourage family members and caregivers to participate in treatment and to provide input for customizing the program to meet the patient's needs. With this input, you can then modify tasks and cuing procedures as needed.

Some of the memory strategies presented in this guide are not appropriate for all persons experiencing memory impairments. You will need to tailor the memory program to meet each individual's needs.

1 Medical Disorders That Result in Memory Impairments

There are numerous medical disorders that cause memory deficits of varying degrees, and memory impairment may be only one of several cognitive skills affected by the disorder. This chapter summarizes some of the disorders that can result in memory impairment.

Cerebrovascular Disorders

The human brain contains over ten billion nerve cells and approximately 20% of the body's total blood supply, and consumes about 25% of the total oxygen used by the body. The human brain requires a continuous supply of oxygen and glucose. If the blood supply is stopped for 2 to 3 minutes, permanent damage to brain tissue will occur (Brookshire 1978).

Chronic Ischemia of the Brain

Reduced blood supply to the brain, or ischemia, can occur as a result of an embolism, thrombosis, vasoconstriction, or atherosclerosis. Atherosclerosis, reduced flow of blood through the arteries due to deposits of cholesterol, is a common cause of brain ischemia. These cholesterol deposits decrease the diameter of the arteries and impede the flow of blood. As the arteries narrow, blood flow to the brain decreases. Cerebral atherosclerosis can result in dementia and strokes. Most individuals with progressive, severe cerebral atherosclerosis will exhibit cognitive impairments.

Atherosclerosis is the most common cause of carotid artery occlusion. One method of treatment, carotid endarterectomy, removes the core of the blocked carotid artery. Increases in verbal comprehension and perceptual organization were observed in 17 patients who underwent carotid endarterectomy (Haynes et al. 1976). Additionally, a decrease in aphasic signs, confusion, and disorientation was documented post surgery.

Transient Ischemic Disorders

Transient ischemic attack (TIA) is a lack of blood flow to a specific area of the brain. This problem is caused by blockage of a vessel resulting in a breakdown in the blood supply system of the brain. This condition can result from a blood clot or a buildup of fat deposits in a vessel. Neurological symptoms depend on the location and severity of the blockage in the brain. Symptoms usually resolve within 24 hours.

The patient experiencing a TIA may notice numbness of fingers, slurred speech, visual impairments, swallowing difficulties, and facial weakness. Cognitively, the patient may experience recent and remote memory deficits and decreased speed for processing information. By definition, TIAs leave no long-lasting impairments.

Multi-Infarct Dementia

Multi-infarct dementia occurs as a result of artery occlusions which cause infarcts (death of tissue) in the cortex and subcortical areas. The location and extent of tissue damage determines the type of deficits manifested (cortical, subcortical, or mixed dementia). Many "ministrokes" may occur throughout the brain.

When small, multiple infarctions in the basal ganglia and pons heal, cavities (called lacunar infarcts) are formed. As the number of lacunar infarctions increases, a progressive dementia develops, which also includes swallowing difficulties, dysarthria, rigidity, and abnormal gait. This lacunar state is characterized by cognitive deficits including recent memory impairments, perseveration, confusion, and slowed thought processes. The severity of the deficits depends on the location and number of infarctions (Khan 1986).

Cerebral Infarctions

The anterior cerebral artery, middle cerebral artery, and posterior cerebral artery are responsible for supplying blood to the brain. Occlusion of one of these major cerebral arteries causes large cerebral infarctions and will result in compromised function for those parts of the brain served by the affected artery. Infarction of the left hemisphere typically causes aphasia and/or apraxia. Right hemisphere infarction produces cognitive deficits which may include disorientation, decreased judgment, memory loss, visual-motor deficits, abnormal prosody of speech, and poor ability to initiate a task.

Angular gyrus syndrome occurs when the posterior portion of the middle cerebral artery is occluded. Clinically, patients' deficits are somewhat similar to those of patients with Alzheimer's disease, with the exception that symptom onset is abrupt. However, individuals with angular gyrus syndrome usually have little difficulty remembering how to complete daily activities and are able to learn new tasks. Spatial orientation generally remains intact. These patients experience varying degrees of expressive and receptive aphasia depending on the location and extent of the lesion.

Posterior cerebral artery occlusions, which produce right-side lesions, may produce environmental/spatial disorientation and facial recognition difficulties. Bilateral occlusions produce severe memory deficits and cortical blindness (Khan 1986).

Head Trauma

Approximately eight to nine million people experience head injuries each year (Karlsberk 1980). Brain damage can occur as a result of the direct impact to the head. Secondary complications such as swelling of the brain, delayed intracranial hemorrhage, intercranial hypertension, and infection can result in further damage to the brain. Head trauma can cause focal, multifocal, and diffuse brain damage.

Focal, Multifocal, and Diffuse Brain Damage

Focal damage refers to a localized lesion of the brain, such as a brain contusion or epidural, subdural, or intracerebral hematoma. Multifocal damage results when several localized lesions of the brain occur. Excessive acceleration or deceleration of the brain within the cranium causes diffuse brain damage. The shaking effect of the impact stretches and tears nerve fibers, causing damage to the nerve cells. In most cases, a head injury causes both diffuse and focal brain injuries (Khan 1986).

Loss of consciousness secondary to head injury is common. The Glasgow Coma Scale (Teasdale and Jennett 1974) was developed to measure the degree of loss of consciousness. It also predicts the length and result of coma. This scale measures three factors (motor response, verbal response, eye opening) that quantitatively relate to consciousness. Higher points are given to responses that indicate increasing degrees of arousal. Generally, the longer the patient is in a coma, the more severe the deficits.

Brain injury can cause physical, perceptual, cognitive, and emotional disabilities. In most cases, memory, attention, and information processing speed and efficiency are the cognitive skills most severely affected as a result of a closed head injury (Capruso and Levin 1992). Cognitive recovery from head injury is slow, and cognitive disorders have been found to have a negative effect on return to employment (Lam, Priddy, and Johnson 1991; Wehman et al. 1989).

Memory Disorders and Head Injury

Most people who experience a traumatic head injury have some degree of memory impairment. Post-traumatic amnesia (PTA) is an inability to remember continuous events after an injury. The person with post-traumatic amnesia has difficulty recalling daily events, answering questions intelligently, and orienting to time and place. During this time of disorientation, the person may experience islands of memory, specific memories of special events or activities that have recently occurred. However, these patients lack the ability to sequence these events temporally. The person may confabulate (fabricate events and information) when unable to recall actual occurrences of events or experiences.

The length of post-traumatic amnesia correlates with the severity of injury. The longer the person experiences post-traumatic amnesia, the more severe the injury and the memory impairment (Brooks 1976, 1980). The person usually experiences lapses of memory to some degree, even when able to recall continuous memories.

Anterograde amnesia refers to the loss of memory of new experiences and information that occurs after an injury. Individuals with head injury perceive anterograde memory deficits as the most problematic type of memory loss (Mateer, Sohlberg, and Crinean 1987). Retrograde amnesia refers to the loss of memory for events before the injury. The duration of retrograde amnesia is measured as the time between the injury and the last clear memory the person recalls prior to the injury. Retrograde amnesia generally exhibits itself as a temporary memory gap of a long period that gradually shrinks during recovery, or a short memory gap period that persists after recovery. The duration of retrograde amnesia is usually short.

Learning new information is generally most difficult for the person with head injury. The ability to recall material that was learned prior to the head injury is usually less impaired. Except for severe cases, immediate recall of information tends to be intact. Delayed recall is most often impaired. Poor attention, poor organizational abilities, and increased cautiousness — all common problems for the population with head injury — negatively affect memory storage. The extent of visual, verbal, and motor memory deficits varies from injury to injury (Khan 1986). The amount and rate of memory recovery post trauma also varies. Recovery tends to occur most rapidly during the first six months post injury (Eson, Yen, and Bourke 1978).

Chronic Central Nervous System Infections

Progressive Multifocal Leukoencephalopathy

Progressive multifocal leukoencephalopathy is a degenerative disorder caused by papovaviruses (one of a group of small viruses that may cause cancer). This disorder occurs primarily in patients with malignant neoplasms such as breast and lung cancer, Hodgkin's disease, lymphosarcoma, and chronic lymphocytic and myelogenous leukemias. The disorder causes demyelination in various areas of the central nervous system. Deficits are related to the location and number of lesions in the brain. Declines in memory, attention, and language skills are exhibited, with death usually occurring in two to four months.

Subacute Sclerosing Panencephalitis

This uncommon disease is caused by a measles or measles-like virus that causes the brain to swell. Degeneration of the neurons in the cortex, basal ganglia, pons, and inferior olives occurs. Onset is gradual. Clinical symptoms of decreased memory and attention, temper outbursts, and restlessness are evident in the early stages. As the disease progresses, usually in a matter of weeks or months, incoordination, ataxia, and reading, writing, and visual impairments are manifested. This condition occurs in children and adolescents and is terminal.

Creutzfeldt-Jakob Disease

This very rare illness is caused by a slow-acting virus that leads to complete brain failure. Death usually occurs within one year and affects individuals primarily between the ages of 40 and 80. Cell loss is observed in the spinal cord, cortex, and basal ganglia. Memory impairments, poor attention, and fatigue are common complaints in the initial stages of the disease. Cognitive and physical deterioration is evident from week to week. As the disease progresses, general intellectual decline, aphasia, apraxia, agnosia, amnesia, and confusion develop. The patient may experience hallucinations and delusions in the final stage of the disease (Khan 1986).

Syphilis

Syphilis is caused by a bacterium that is transmitted through contact with an infectious lesion. In the early stages, small red bumps on the skin appear and lymph nodes become inflamed. Paralysis, tremors, seizures, dysarthria, ataxia, apraxia, and aphasia occur if the disease is left untreated. Memory impairments (recent memory) and poor judgment tend to be the first cognitive signs of syphilis. As the disease progresses, the patient begins to confabulate, and recent and remote memory becomes increasingly impaired. Psychiatric disorders are common in the end stages of the disease. Prognosis can be favorable if the patient is treated with penicillin. In a study of 200 elderly patients with dementia or psychiatric illness, 1% were found to have untreated central nervous system syphilis (Kra 1986).

Bacterial Meningitis in Children

At least one-fourth of the children who had meningeal infections in childhood experience long-term effects secondary to brain damage. Memory, attention, and language deficits are common. With the mortality rate from bacterial meningitis decreasing, there is an increase in survivors left with cognitive deficits. A study of 50 children who recovered from bacterial meningitis revealed that 50% of the children showed no deficits, 9% displayed behavioral problems, and 28% experienced significant handicaps such as mental retardation, hearing impairments, language disorders, motor deficits, seizures, and visual impairments (Sell 1983).

Acquired Immune Deficiency Syndrome (AIDS)

AIDS is a disease that attacks the body's defenses against infection. It is caused by a virus and is thought to be spread through the exchange of body fluids. Initial symptoms may include fatigue, swollen lymph glands, loss of appetite, weight loss, nonspecific gastrointestinal symptoms, and depression. As the disease progresses, fatigue increases and patients are prone to pneumocystis carinii, a form of pneumonia. Many patients also develop meningitis, encephalitis, and several types of cancer including non-Hodgkin's lymphoma, Kaposi's sarcoma, and Burkitt's lymphoma (Glanze, Anderson, and Anderson 1985). Cerebrovascular disease is also quite common in patients with AIDS (Grundman et al. 1989).

Two-thirds of all persons with AIDS experience neurologic symptoms during their lifetime, and about 10% of all patients present with a neurologic complaint as their first symptom (Rosenblum, Levy, and Bredesen 1988). The majority of patients with AIDS develop severe global intellectual impairments. A significant number of patients will experience mild to moderate intellectual impairments for four to seven months before the onset of severe intellectual impairments. Early cognitive symptoms include confusion, loss of concentration, forgetfulness, and slowness of thought. Some persons experience motor impairments such as hypertonia, quadriparesis or paraparesis, and ataxia with only minimal intellectual deficits (Grundman et al. 1989).

Degenerative Diseases
of the Nervous System

Individuals with degenerative diseases will have various degrees of memory and cognitive impairments, depending on the stage of the illness. The person may be able to remember past events without difficulty but is unable to recall what has just happened. Memory aids may assist these people in maintaining their independence in the early stages of the disease. External memory strategies (such as memory books and visual environmental cues) tend to be more beneficial for some of these patients than teaching them internal strategies (mnemonics). In the later stages of the disease, memory aid use may become more frustrating than beneficial. Each individual's abilities and needs should be assessed before prescribing a memory program.

Cortical dementia refers to cognitive changes secondary to diseases that affect the cortex, such as Alzheimer's disease and Pick's disease. The motor system, for the most part, is spared. These patients show little or no difficulty moving their muscles or walking. Language, visuospatial, and cognitive skills are most impaired. On the other hand, subcortical dementia affects primarily muscle movements, resulting in poor posture and decreased muscle tone and ability to walk. Secondary deficits include language difficulties and cognitive impairments.

Alzheimer's Disease

An estimated 2.4 to 2.8 million people in the United States have Alzheimer's disease. The cause of senile dementia of the Alzheimer's type is unknown. Several theories on the cause of this type of dementia have been suggested, including aluminum intoxication, viral diseases, immunological defects, and genetic factors.

Research has shown that individuals with Alzheimer's disease have a deficiency of choline acetyltransferase, an enzyme that is required in the production of the neurotransmitter acetylcholine. Somatostatin, another neurotransmitter, has also been found to be deficient in individuals with Alzheimer's disease. It appears that cell loss occurs at the site in the brain where acetylcholine originates, the nucleus basalis of Meynert. Brain tissue biopsies have also revealed abnormal quantities of neuritic plaques and neurofibrillary tangles in the brain tissue of patients with Alzheimer's disease (Kra 1986).

A physician makes a diagnosis of Alzheimer's disease after examining symptoms, ruling out other causes for the symptoms, documenting the progression of symptoms over time, and obtaining compatible CT or nuclear magnetic resonance (NMR) imaging test results.

Seven stages of Alzheimer's disease have been described (Reisberg et al. 1982).

Stage 1: no cognitive impairments

Stage 2: slight decrease in functional memory skills. Memory tests may or may not reveal a mild impairment. The patient may occasionally forget the name of a friend or well-known person. The patient may or may not be aware of slight changes in memory skills. Employment is not negatively affected.

Stage 3: mild cognitive deficits. The patient may begin to lose items, become lost in unfamiliar locations, demonstrate increased anxiety, have difficulty recalling verbal information, and exhibit decreased ability to attend to tasks. The patient generally denies symptoms.

Stage 4: continued decline of cognitive skills. The patient demonstrates decreased recall of general knowledge. The patient is oriented to place and is able to recognize familiar friends and family members. Pathfinding for well-known places is intact. The patient is unable to complete complex tasks, and attention is noticeably impaired. The patient may continue to deny symptoms.

Stage 5: moderately severe cognitive impairments. The patient is generally able to recall the names of immediate family members and complete personal care with occasional cues. Because of the patient's poor judgment, it is unsafe to leave the person alone. The patient is unable to answer biographical and temporal orientation questions accurately (for example: How many children do you have? Where do your children live? What is your address? What is today's date? What time is it?).

Stage 6: severe cognitive impairments. The patient may show some knowledge of surroundings. The patient is able to recall own name. The person may be able to complete simple routine tasks such as cleaning the table. The patient may be unable to recall the names of spouse and children, recall recent experiences, or maintain a train of thought. Assistance for daily living activities is needed. The patient may exhibit delusional and/or violent behaviors and may become easily agitated.

Stage 7: severe cognitive deficits. This stage is classified as late dementia. The patient may be totally nonverbal, phonating only occasionally. Loss of all basic functions (including urinary continence, self-feeding, and walking) characterizes this final stage.

There is no standard length of time that the patient with Alzheimer's disease remains in a particular stage. Some patients progress rapidly from one stage to the next; others remain in the early stages for decades before deteriorating to later stages.

Pick's Disease

This is a degenerative disease similar to Alzheimer's disease, causing severe cognitive deficits. (Alzheimer's disease occurs 10 to 15 times more frequently than Pick's disease.) Onset usually occurs between 40 and 60 years of age. Pick's disease causes atrophy of the brain, most commonly in the temporal and/or frontal lobes. Patients with this disease develop a ravenous appetite, loss of fear, oral exploratory behavior, and hypersexuality, and tend to demand to explore environmental stimuli as soon as they are perceived. Aphasia usually develops in the early stages of the disease, but memory and visuospatial skills are intact until the middle or later stages. In the end stages of the disease, all cognitive, motor, and visuospatial skills are impaired. Death generally occurs 6 to 12 years after onset; only 20% of the patients live longer than 10 years.

Parkinson's Disease

The symptoms of Parkinson's disease occur most frequently between the ages of 50 and 70. The course of this slow, progressive disease is variable. Death results most often in the later stages of the disease when the patient is confined to bed rest. Death is usually a result of respiratory and urinary complications.

Loss of nerve cells occurs in the basal ganglia with deficient amounts of dopamine, a chemical messenger that sends signals from one nerve cell to another. Atrophy is found throughout the cerebral cortex, especially in the frontal lobes, and is similar to that found in Alzheimer's patients. Tremors affect about two-thirds of the patients. The tremors tend to increase when the patient is relaxed. Spontaneous movement becomes increasingly difficult, with gradual loss of the ability to initiate movements. Loss of facial expression occurs. Patients' speech is commonly monotone with reduced volume. Drooling and swallowing difficulties may develop. Aphasia, apraxia, and agnosia develop in some cases. Depression is common.

Cognitive deficits become apparent as the disease progresses. Verbal and visual memory skills, calculation, abstract reasoning, and concept formation skills decline. Patients may become extremely forgetful.

Progressive Supranuclear Palsy

These patients exhibit symptoms that are similar to those produced by Parkinson's disease: gait difficulties, postural instability, loss of facial expression, dysarthria, and rigidity of neck and upper trunk. Additionally, these patients exhibit vertical gaze difficulties. Thought processes are slowed, and difficulties with calculation, attention, and abstract reasoning are common. Forgetfulness is most often due to poor attention skills. Remote memories are generally intact if the person is given enough time to respond to questions. Verbal and perceptual skills are most often spared. Apathy and other personality changes are common early in the disease. Cognitive deficits, including memory impairments, are generally mild and develop in the later stages of the disease.

Wilson's Disease

This is a rare genetic illness that results from excessive copper deposits in the brain, liver, and kidneys. Damage of the basal ganglia, cerebral cortex, and cerebellum can be seen. There are two forms of Wilson's disease: the acute form which begins in late childhood or adolescence; and the chronic form, referred to as pseudosclerosis.

The characteristics of the acute form include dystonia, slurring of speech, swallowing difficulties, rigidity, and spasticity. The chronic form of the disease is marked by wrist or arm tremors, altered kidney and liver functions, and progressive head and trunk involvement. Treatment with the chemical D-penicillamine effectively removes copper from the body with good clinical results over time.Cognitively, these patients exhibit memory impairments, slowed thought processing, and decreased conceptual thinking. Cognitive skills improve with the treatment of D-penicillamine.

Huntington's Disease

This is a rare degenerative disease that develops in adulthood. Short, rapid jerks of isolated muscles (chorea), including bending and extending the fingers and raising and lowering the shoulders, are characteristic of the disease. Spasms of the neck, lips, tongue, and cheeks are common, along with marked clumsiness and abnormal gait pattern. Chewing and swallowing food is difficult for these patients. Rigidity and akinesia may develop early in some patients instead of chorea.

Personality changes are evident, usually prior to the development of chorea. These patients may become aggressive, easily angered, and moody. Untidiness and loss of motivation for work and social activities have also been observed. A schizophrenia-like syndrome occurs in approximately one-third of these patients prior to developing chorea.

In the early stages of the disease, remote and recent memory recall has been found to be of primary difficulty (Albert, Butters, and Brandt 1981; Butters, Albert, and Sax 1979). Patients' attention is usually intact. These patients tend to have difficulty generating ideas, initiating tasks, planning and organizing activities, and following through on tasks. These patients are able to complete highly structured activities with minimal cues.

Idiopathic Calcification of Basal Ganglia

This familial disorder with onset in infancy or in adult life is marked by calcification of the basal ganglia. Patients develop a movement disorder similar to Parkinson's disease, and cognitive and emotional changes occur. As the disease progresses, recent memory skills become impaired, attention decreases, and abstract reasoning skills decline. Depression, delusions, and hallucinations occur in some cases.

Spinocerebellar Degeneration

Spinocerebellar degeneration comprises a group of hereditary diseases that involve the spinal structures, basal ganglia, brain stem, and cerebellum, in varying degrees. Friedreich's ataxia is included in this classification. In this disorder, a breakdown of the spinal cord occurs with possible involvement of brain nerve tracts. Friedreich's ataxia usually affects individuals between 5 and 20 years of age. Cognitive impairments are occasionally observed but are highly variable in spinocerebellar degeneration.

Hallervorden-Spatz Syndrome

Hallervorden-Spatz syndrome is thought to be an autosomal recessive genetic disease producing dystonia and athetosis. Onset can occur in late infancy, childhood, or adulthood. There is cortical involvement in the frontal and temporal regions. This disease is terminal, and a decline in cognitive and memory skills occurs in the majority of cases. A decrease in attention, abstract reasoning, judgment, and visual-spatial skills is gradual. Paranoid schizophrenia and mental confusion have been documented in several cases.

Chronic Diseases

Lack of Oxygen

The brain requires oxygen to function. Lack of oxygen (hypoxemia) impairs the cerebral metabolism, which leads to cognitive deficits such as memory impairments, poor judgment, decreased attention, and slow mental processing. A lack of oxygen can be caused by:

- insufficient oxygen present in the air
- inability of the oxygen to reach the respiratory tract (a result of muscular weakness, neurological disorders, respiratory arrest, or neuromuscular blocking agents)
- inability of the oxygen to pass through the lung tissue (as in chronic lung disease)

- decreased ability of the blood to carry oxygen (as in anemia or carbon monoxide poisoning) (Kra 1986)
- lack of oxygen reaching the brain tissue (such as occurs during cardiac arrest or cardiac diseases)

The severity of cognitive impairment varies according to the rate and duration of oxygen deprivation. Generally, acute oxygen deprivation of considerable duration results in extensive brain damage and severe cognitive impairment. Chronic oxygen deprivation slowly produces cognitive and personality changes such as impaired recent memory, increased irritability, and lack of motivation (Khan 1986).

Lung Diseases

Patients with chronic lung disorders (such as chronic bronchitis and emphysema) exhibit cognitive changes including memory loss. These impairments are reversible if pulmonary functions improve (Krop, Block, and Cohn 1973).

Cardiac Diseases

Lack of blood reaching the brain tissue appears to be related to cardiac output. Patients with cardiac diseases may exhibit memory loss, confusion, and decreased attention. Congestive heart failure, aortic stenosis, and mitral stenosis can cause cognitive impairments. If medical treatment is initiated and cardiac output is restored, cognitive skills generally improve. Cerebrovascular complication after open-heart surgery is fairly common. It is estimated that approximately 5% experience strokes, and 30% to 40% of all open-heart surgery patients experience residual cognitive impairments that may last for months or longer (Kra 1986).

Anemia

Oxygen binds with hemoglobin in the blood and is carried to the brain cells. The term *anemia* refers to a deficiency of hemoglobin, red blood cells, or both, or a loss of blood volume. Anemia can occur when important nutrients such as iron or vitamins are deficient in the body or when there is actual blood loss from the body. In an elderly patient with already compromised cognitive skills, anemia can negatively affect cognitive skills even further. The neurological condition tends to clear up promptly when proper medical treatment is given for the anemia.

Chronic Renal Failure

The kidney recycles waste materials in the body, manufactures hormones, and helps keep the concentrations of proteins and salts in balance. Patients experiencing renal failure demonstrate decreased attention, memory, and reasoning skills (Ginn 1975; Lederman and Henry 1978). Confusion, agitation, hallucinations, and verbal outbursts have been noted. Elderly individuals with renal disorders tend to be more prone to cognitive and emotional changes.

Kidney failure, or uremia, can be caused by chronic infections; immunological disturbances; abnormal deposits of amyloid, calcium, and uric acid; injuries; cancer; or compromised blood supply. Medications such as kanamycin, gentamicin, polymyxin B, colymycin, streptomycin, vancomycin, para-aminosalicylic acid, amphotericin B, amikacin, and tobramycin have been found to cause kidney failure in some patients. One of the initial signs of kidney failure is fatigue. If kidney failure is untreated, the patient becomes disoriented, falls into a coma, and dies (Kra 1986).

Dialysis dementia is a progressive condition characterized by cognitive decline, speech disturbances, myoclonic jerks, seizures, and psychological symptoms. These symptoms have been reported by numerous dialysis centers. The cause of this dementia is unknown, and no correlation has been made between age of patient, cause of kidney failure, type of dialysis used, or duration of dialysis (Khan 1986).

Chronic Liver Diseases

Cirrhosis and other chronic liver diseases can cause brain tissue damage. These diseases can produce decreased attention, impaired recent memory, psychiatric disorders (sometimes the first clinical sign of a problem), and coma. Anterograde and retrograde amnesia have been documented in cases of prolonged comas (Summerskill, Davidson, and Sherlock 1956). It appears that cognitive and mental changes are due to cerebral intoxication by intestinal contents that the liver is unable to metabolize.

Hyperthyroidism

The thyroid gland secretes the hormones thyroxine and tri-iodothyronine. The thyroid relies on iodine obtained from foods to produce these hormones, which regulate the metabolism of the body. An overactive thyroid produces a condition called Grave's disease or thyrotoxicosis, causing tremors, swelling in the neck, weight loss, increased appetite, nervousness, and sometimes psychosis. Cognitive impairments including poor attention and recent memory deficits have been documented (Whybrow, Prange, and Treadway 1969; Robbins and Vinson 1960).

Hypothyroidism

Hypothyroidism is a condition marked by decreased activity of the thyroid gland. This condition can be caused by an overdose of antithyroid medicine, atrophy of the gland itself, or a decrease in levels of thyroid-stimulating hormone from the pituitary gland. Left untreated, hypothyroidism results in coma and death. In the early stages, these patients experience slowing of their mental functions. As the condition progresses, they demonstrate poor concentration and decreased abstract reasoning and memory skills. Long-standing hypothyroidism may lead to dementia and psychosis (Whybrow, Prange, and Treadway 1969). Cognitive skills tend to improve with treatment (Schon, Sutherland, and Rawson 1961).

Cushing's Syndrome

Cushing's syndrome is a disorder that results from large amounts of adrenocorticotropic hormone being released by the pituitary gland; it can also be caused by large doses of steroid drugs over a period of weeks or longer. Memory impairments, decreased attention, and intellectual disturbances are characteristic. Approximately half of the patients experience psychiatric symptoms, which frequently disappear with treatment.

Addison's Disease

This disease is caused by partial or complete failure of the adrenal gland as a result of autoimmune diseases, infection, tumor, or bleeding of the gland. The disease occurs midlife and affects men more frequently than women. Symptoms include decreased attention, restlessness, irritability, recent and remote memory impairments, periods of confusion, disorientation, irritability, and mood changes.

Electrolyte and Fluid Disturbances

To use energy, the body must have the correct amounts of the main electrolytes. Chronic diseases of the heart, adrenal gland, kidney, and liver and the use of some drugs may lead to the lack of one or more electrolytes and cause fluid disturbances.

Older adults tend to be sensitive to electrolyte and fluid disturbances. Decreased attention, impaired recent memory, disorientation, and occasionally psychosis are symptoms of electrolyte and fluid disturbances. Hypernatremia (an overconcentration of sodium in the blood as a result of dehydration) can cause the brain to shrink, producing confusion, even coma. Acute hyponatremia is caused by excessive drinking or from administration of excessive amounts of intravenous fluids. In acute cases, brain edema can result. Lethargy, memory impairments, and decreased cognitive functions are exhibited by patients with hyponatremia (Khan 1986).

Diabetes

Diabetes is caused (1) by the failure of the pancreas to release enough insulin in the body or (2) by a defect in the cells that accept the insulin, making the hormone ineffective in regulating blood sugar levels. Patients who have elevated blood sugar levels will often experience memory loss, confusion, generalized weakness, and lethargy. Prolonged dementia can result if blood sugar levels fall too low. Treatment focuses on maintaining a sugar and insulin balance by controlling the diet, or by administering insulin tablets or injections (Kra 1986).

Developmental Disorders

A developmental disorder is any condition that hinders individuals from reaching their full potential. Developmental disorders include language impairments, motor handicaps, sensory deficits, cognitive disorders, and disorders of social functioning. Genetic influences, prenatal events, and perinatal events can cause a broad range of disorders. Learning disorders and mental retardation are two of the most common developmental disorders.

Learning Disorders

Learning disorders affect 5% to 20% of school-aged children. Males are affected six to eight times more frequently than females (Colwell 1984).

The concept of learning disabilities is relatively new. The term is used to describe a disorder in one or more of the processes involved in using language. Learning disabilities can become apparent in disorders of listening, thinking, talking, reading, spelling, or arithmetic. The definition describes children of normal intelligence with processing difficulties who do not perform as well as expected in school. Several areas of development which appear to be important in achieving success in school have been identified: memory, sequencing ability, visual-spatial skills, fine and gross motor skills, and selective attention (Levine, Brooks, and Shonkoff 1980).

Attention Deficit Disorders

Attention deficit disorders have recently created much attention in the field of education. The clinical features of children with attention deficit disorder (ADD) are inattention, impulsivity, and hyperactivity inappropriate for the child's developmental level. Motor hyperactivity is seen in these children across all social settings (Golden 1992). One study found that 6% of all public elementary school students were receiving drug treatment for hyperactivity and inattentiveness (Safer and Krager 1988). Research has also found that children with ADD continue to experience symptoms of the disorder into adulthood (Weiss and Hechtman 1985; Gittleman-Klein et al. 1985). The clinical features of ADD can negatively affect learning and success in school and subsequent employment.

Mental Retardation

Mental retardation is a disorder characterized by below-average intelligence with problems in the ability to learn and to interact socially. This disorder occurs more often in males than females, and the severity of retardation varies. IQ measures are used to determine the severity of the disorder.

Aging

Biological Changes

As the brain ages, biological changes occur. Cell death, metabolic changes, decreased oxygen supply, and changes in neuronal communication occur with aging. These biological changes have been studied to determine the effect of aging on brain functions (Khan 1986).

Recent studies reveal that neuronal loss with age is only minimal (Terry et al. 1981). In the cerebral cortex, dendritic spines (branches that extend from the dendrites of most neurons) are a common site of synaptic contact. Neuronal input can be reduced or lost if a change in density or structure of the dendritic spines occurs. Degenerative changes of the dendrites and dendritic spines do occur as the brain ages. However, the potential to develop new spines is not lost with age. Some studies have even shown dendrite and dendritic spine growth in some older individuals (Buell and Coleman 1979).

Other biological changes that occur in the brain with aging include an increase in water content of cells, increased rigidity of the neuronal membrane, alterations in neurotransmitter concentrations, reduction of enzymes, lower cholinergic receptor binding in the cerebral cortex, and metabolic rate changes. However, some of these alterations appear to be variable. Currently, there is no evidence that these biological changes are directly related to memory impairments in individuals who are elderly (Khan 1986).

Memory Studies

Memory complaints are common among older adults. Studies designed to identify the type and severity of memory decline with age have produced contradictory findings. A more rapid decay of visual sensory memory, and to a lesser extent auditory sensory memory, has been demonstrated in older individuals (Schonfield and Wenger 1975; Walsh and Thompson 1978; Clark and Knowles 1973). However, it is generally agreed that there is no substantial difference between older adults and younger individuals in their ability to identify brief sensory stimulus (Ciocon and Potter 1988). Also, differences in short-term memory skills for a series of digits or words have not been consistently demonstrated in studies of older and younger individuals: some studies show no differences in memory span (Craik 1968), while other studies show a slight decline with age (Taub 1973; Botwinick and Storandt 1974).

It does appear that older individuals have more difficulty acquiring and retrieving new information from long-term memory. Some research indicates that, compared to younger subjects, older individuals require increased time to process information in short-term memory, and require greater time to recall the information. Craik (1977) proposes that slowed processing is due to the use of less optimal processing strategies by older adults.

Because memory complaints in older individuals are so common, and because older adults tend to overestimate their forgetfulness, it is important to determine if the client's skills are within normal limits for that age or if the person is experiencing early signs of dementia. It should be kept in mind that neuropsychologic tests are of limited use in the beginning stages of dementia. These tests can provide a baseline of the patient's cognitive skills for comparison with future test results, to rule out significant cognitive decline over time (Ciocon and Potter 1988).

Several factors (including anxiety, depression, and failure to use specific learning strategies frequently employed by younger individuals) appear to have a negative effect on memory function in older adults. Memory training programs designed to assist older individuals in compensating for their memory complaints have proven to influence mental performance and improve self-esteem (Ciocon and Potter 1988; Johnston and Gueldner 1989).

It is important to examine each individual's needs and lifestyle when developing a memory training program and to obtain input from the individual when customizing an external memory system. In a recent study, individuals 20, 45, and 65 years of age were asked to indicate if they owned each of thirty different commercial memory aids and to rate their usefulness. Each age group seemed to use certain memory aids that they felt were useful. Younger adults viewed "high-tech" aids such as electronic memo pads and videocassette recorders as being useful memory aids, whereas older adults viewed aids to assist them with daily life needs as being useful. The authors suggest that memory tasks change with age and life-stage changes, and therefore the usefulness of different memory aids also changes (Petro et al. 1991).

When assisting clients in establishing memory aid systems, it is important to investigate each client's needs in that person's specific environment. Observing a patient in the home and work environments, interviewing family and caregivers, and communicating with other professionals involved in the patient's care will give the clinician valuable information about the patient's needs. It is important to remember that some patients may deny or minimize their memory deficits. Observing the patient complete daily living tasks and simulated functional tasks will help the clinician develop an accurate clinical picture of the patient's skills.

Alcoholism

Although chronic alcohol consumption has detrimental effects on all body organs, the nervous system appears to be the most sensitive to alcohol. Alcohol consumption can cause cognitive and memory deficits. The brain's sensitivity to alcohol varies. Severe brain damage can occur after 10 to 15 years of chronic drinking in moderate to heavy amounts (Khan 1986).

Patients who go through treatment and abstain from alcohol consumption do show signs of cognitive recovery in the first week of abstinence, with maximal improvement at four to eight weeks (Guthrie et al. 1980). Brain damage is permanent in severe cases. Progressive brain atrophy, cortical shrinkage, ventricular enlargement, and a significant reduction in brain weight can occur as a result of chronic alcohol abuse (Khan 1986). Korsakoff syndrome is the name given to the permanent progressive memory deterioration that results from chronic drinking. These patients are usually disoriented and provide false information to conceal their memory problems.

2 The Brain and Memory

Organization of Memory

Researchers have given much attention to memory, a specific process or activity that takes place in the central nervous system as a result of environmental input. No one structure in the brain has been identified as being solely responsible for memory.

Damage to the cortex of the brain results in some loss of learning and memory. Memory impairments have resulted from temporal lobe tumors, third ventricle tumors, lesions of the midbrain reticular formation, and damage to the hippocampus and the mammillary bodies (Simma 1955; Williams and Pennybacker 1954; Grunthal 1947; Scoville and Milner 1957; Penfield and Milner 1958).

Types of Memory

Research tends to focus on the characteristics of various forms of memory and their relationship to each other. Much of what has been learned about memory is a result of studies of patients with memory impairments, subjects of normal health and mental ability, and related studies with experimental animals. Numerous theories have been proposed to explain memory processes. Atkinson and Shiffrin (1968) divided memory into three components: sensory memory, short-term memory, and long-term memory.

Sensory Memory

Sensory memory is the first impression of incoming sensory information. The smell of perfume, the image of a face, or the sound of a voice is received by the sensory organs. Once the stimulation ceases, the impression is either lost over time or it is processed to be remembered later. This initial processing is thought to be carried out by brief sensory-memory stores (Craik 1979). This first impression is short-lived, lasting from 250 milliseconds to as long as 80 seconds, depending on the sensory modality (visual, auditory, tactile, olfactory, or kinesthetic) (Khan 1986).

Iconic memory refers to visual representation (icon meaning symbol or image), and echoic memory refers to auditory impressions. There is no memory storage label to describe touch, taste, or smell. These sensory memories last briefly and allow individuals to interpret and integrate sensory input into meaningful information (Wilson 1987b).

Short-Term Memory

Sensory information or sensory memory is transferred to short-term memory, also called primary memory, immediate memory, span memory, and working memory (Kelly 1964; Shiffrin and Schneider 1977). The format of the information is visual (remembering pictures and images) as well as verbal (Khan 1986).

Short-term memory, which actually refers to how many items can be perceived at one time, has a limited capacity of approximately seven items for most people. There does not seem to be any significant difference in short-term memory capacity between younger and older adults (Poon 1985).

The information in short-term memory is displaced by new incoming information or is lost by decay with time. Rehearsal (repeating the information over and over) allows the information to stay in short-term memory so it can be coded, transferred, and stored in long-term memory. Experiences that are not coded or processed and then transferred for permanent storage become irretrievable (Postman 1975; Reitman 1971).

It is generally agreed that short-term memory and long-term memory are distinguishable (Glanzer and Cunitz 1966; Atkinson and Shiffrin 1968). Amnesic patients can have intact short-term memory but demonstrate severely impaired long-term memory (Cave and Squire 1992). In another study, subjects with short-term memory deficits (as measured by digit span) did not demonstrate a deficit in verbal long-term memory (Shallice and Warrington 1970). Differentiation of short-term and long-term memory has also been demonstrated in animal experiments.

Long-Term Memory

Long-term memory, also called long-term store, secondary memory, and distant memory, is a permanent record of information learned and experiences of the past. Long-term memory has a larger storage capacity (possibly unlimited), and information can be retained for a lifetime. External memory aids and memory strategies are designed to teach people to compensate for long-term memory deficits.

Tulving (1972) refers to two types of long-term memory: semantic and episodic. Semantic memory involves remembering factual information such as definitions of words and semantic relationships and is not dependent on time or place. For example, three feet make a yard. This memory is not dependent on who told you this information, or when or where you learned it.

Episodic memories are given spatial and temporal codes. Remembering personal events such as one's wedding day, what one did on the last birthday, or when one's rent check was sent are examples of episodic memories.

Procedural memory and prospective memory are two types of long-term memory that have been identified. Procedural memory involves remembering the procedure for completing a task or doing a job. This skill is important for teaching memory book system use. Prospective memory is the type of memory required to carry out actions in the future. One study indicated that prospective memory deficits were viewed as the most problematic for patients (Mateer, Sohlberg, and Crinean 1987). Memory book systems teach patients to compensate for prospective memory deficits. Remembering appointments, work schedules, things to do, medication schedules, and other such information is important for independent living. If a patient can learn to compensate for prospective memory problems, the person's level of independence may be increased and the need for supervision decreased.

When You Fail to Remember

There are several theories that attempt to explain why individuals are unable to recall previously learned information. One theory proposes that time decays the memory trace. According to this theory, spontaneous degeneration occurs if information is not used. Another theory suggests that previously learned information interferes with new learning (proactive inhibition) and that new learning interferes with something learned in the past (retroactive inhibition). Another explanation of forgetting suggests that the information once learned is not lost or forgotten, but that there is difficulty with the retrieval process. If the appropriate cue is provided, the apparently forgotten information may be recalled successfully (Higbee 1977b).

Improving Memory Skills

There appear to be two broad approaches to memory skill training (Glisky and Schacter 1986). The first approach attempts to restore memory function, focusing on activities such as memorizing word lists, recalling details in paragraphs, and other exercises and drills aimed at restoring memory function. However, these activities generally fail to affect patients' memory needs outside the treatment environment or to improve memory scores on formal tests (Godfrey and Knight 1985; Schacter, Rich, and Stamp 1985).

The second approach to memory training is designed to help patients compensate for their memory deficits. Clinicians train patients to use internal and external memory strategies in therapy and then to generalize this skill to the home, school, and work environments. Treatment focuses on teaching individuals to use mnemonic, organization, rehearsal, and written memory strategies. Successful use of these strategies has been documented in numerous studies (Cermak 1975; Crovitz 1979; Wilson 1981, 1982; Sohlberg and Mateer 1989; Bourgeois 1992).

3 Treatment Strategies for Memory Impairments

A Review of the Literature

Memory Improvement

"Will my memory improve?"

Clinicians are frequently asked this question when working with individuals who have memory difficulties. If a memory impairment is due to a treatable medical condition such as hypothyroidism, Cushing's syndrome, cardiac diseases, or others, recovery of memory and associated cognitive deficits generally occurs once appropriate medical treatment is implemented. However, if the memory impairment is caused by irreversible damage to the brain, recovery may be extremely slow and only partial.

Immediate memory span, which is least affected by brain injury, may recover to premorbid levels within three years post injury. Yet there seems to be a significant deterioration on complex immediate memory and retention tasks at approximately two years post injury (Lezak 1979). It appears that changes in brain tissue or metabolic processes occur after injury that are detrimental to recovery (Devor 1982; Lezak 1979).

There are several explanations for the recovery of memory skills. Restoration of function due to dendritic and axonal sprouting may occur in the central nervous system (Glees and Cole 1950). Scar tissue often restricts this sprouting, and sprouting may also occur from intact cells to a denervated region, which could result in spasticity (McCough et al. 1958). Although there is evidence that axonal sprouting occurs, there is no evidence that neuronal growth is stimulated by cognitive retraining tasks (Harris 1984).

Another theory of how memory functions recover is that the healthy brain tissue takes over the function for the damaged areas of the brain, as in the case of recovery of language function (Cummings et al. 1979). However, this seems unlikely, because verbal memory skills generally do not show a gradual recovery, and memory is not specifically localized, as language is (Harris 1984).

Most recovery from memory deficits appears to come from developing strategies using patients' strengths to compensate for a particular deficit. Evidence does not seem to support attempts to retrain memory processes even though therapists use this method in attempting to improve memory (Harris and Sunderland 1981). Memory practice exercises aimed at improving memory performance have been of little benefit for subjects of normal ability nor for patients with memory impairments (Ericsson, Chase, and Falcon 1980; Milner, Corkin, and Teuber 1968; Brooks and Baddeley 1976).

Compensatory Memory Strategies

Memory deficits are a common sequela of a variety of neurological and medical conditions and usually comprise only one of the deficits exhibited. Problems with cognitive, language, visual, and motor skills may also result. Rarely do individuals with brain damage demonstrate memory problems only, without other deficits. Severe functional limitations resulting from memory deficits may exist despite the preservation of other skill areas (Gianutsos and Grynbaum 1983).

Studies on employment after brain injury have revealed that memory and cognitive deficits are the most frequently occurring deficits among unemployed individuals with brain injury. This suggests that these deficits contribute to the high post-injury unemployment rates (Wehman et al. 1989).

Rehabilitation professionals have attempted to teach patients to compensate for their memory deficits in order to increase patients' abilities to function more independently in the community and at home, school, and work. There are generally two types of compensatory memory strategies that are taught in memory training programs: internal memory strategies and external memory strategies.

Internal Memory Strategies

Internal memory strategies are organized mental systems that are used to improve memory. These strategies are commonly referred to as mnemonics (ne MON iks). Mnemonics add something to the information being taught to make it more memorable. These strategies can be either visual or verbal and require a considerable effort on the part of the learner. Using mnemonics can be more interesting than rote learning and therefore make it easier for the learner to attend to the information being memorized (Higbee 1988).

Learning Lists of Items

STORYTELLING. Storytelling, also called link mnemonics and story mnemonics, can be used to aid in remembering lists. A story is used to associate items in a continuous, related sequence. Most people find it easier to recall a story than a series of unrelated words, especially if the words need to be recalled in a specific order (Roediger 1980; Bugelski 1977).

This technique could be used to remember functional items such as grocery lists or lists of things to do. However, most people prefer to use external memory aids (such as shopping lists or "to do" lists) to complete these tasks (Harris 1980). Storytelling techniques may be most effective for students who are required to remember lists of names, events, equations, main points of a textbook chapter, or oral reports. An example of this strategy to complete a functional task is given here:

Errands to be completed:

✔ 1. Go to the store and buy milk.

✔ 2. Pick up shoes at the repair shop.

✔ 3. Pick up dry cleaning.

✔ 4. Buy nails at the hardware store.

Key words to represent each task:

✔ 1. milk   ✔ 3. dry cleaning

✔ 2. shoes   ✔ 4. nails

Story: Some milk spilled on my shoes, so I took them to the dry cleaner, where they nailed the soles together.

This verbal mnemonic system can be effective for individuals who have difficulty using visual imagery. However, some individuals may find that this technique is more powerful if they can picture the events (or draw pictures) as they say the story.

LOCI MNEMONICS. The use of this strategy involves two steps: visualizing a series of locations in logical order, then visualizing each of the items to be remembered on the list at each specific location. The same set of locations can be used over and over again with new lists so that new locations do not need to be learned each time the strategy is used. The location set should be concrete and familiar to the individual using the strategy.

When the list of items is to be recalled, the individual visualizes the memorized location and recalls the image of the item at that location. For example, a patient may choose the location set to be a familiar route: the driveway to the house, the front steps of the house, the front door, the living room couch. The items on the list are then visualized at each location. A patient trying to remember a list of grocery items consisting of milk, cheese, lettuce, and hamburger would then visualize each item at each memorized location.

This technique has been shown to be useful for subjects of normal ability as well as subjects with memory impairments (Robertson-Tchabo, Hausman, and Arenberg 1976; Wilson 1987e; Yesavage and Rose 1984). Elderly individuals tend to have more difficulty recalling locations than younger adults; therefore this strategy may not be as effective as other strategies for older adults (Higbee 1977a). However, studies have indicated that this strategy can be effectively used by persons who are elderly (Yesavage and Rose 1984; Anschutz et al. 1985).

PEG MNEMONICS. Peg mnemonics requires the learner to memorize a set of standard peg words (concrete nouns). Peg words are like mental pegs or hooks on which items to be remembered can be "hung." Once the standard peg words are memorized, the learner associates further items to be remembered with each peg word. Groninger (1971) demonstrated that it takes subjects less time to learn information using peg mnemonics than using no strategy.

RHYMING PEG METHOD. There are several variations of the peg mnemonic strategy. The rhyming peg method uses standard peg words which rhyme with numbers. The learner memorizes the standard set of peg words and associates words to be remembered with each peg word to form a visual image. The following is a list of standard peg words:

one — sun	*four* — shore	*eight* — crate
two — shoe	*five* — hive	*nine* — vine
three — tree	*six* — sticks	*ten* — men
	seven — heaven	

A person wanting to remember four errands to complete during the day would associate the errands with the first four peg words. Assume, for example, that the individual needed to go to the dry cleaner to pick up a shirt, get the oil changed in his car, get his watch repaired, then pick up a pair of glasses. The following is an example of how this strategy would be used:

Peg Word	Errand to be Remembered	Visual Image
One — Sun	Get shirt at dry cleaners	Sun drying shirt
Two — Shoe	Get oil changed	Mechanic's shoes under car
Three — Tree	Get watch repaired	Watch hanging on tree branch
Four — Shore	Pick up glasses	Glasses on the seashore

Visual images should be pictured as vividly as possible. It may also be helpful to draw a picture of the image. One problem with rhyming peg mnemonics is that it is difficult to think of peg words for numbers greater than ten. However, it is possible to remember more than one set of items at a time using this method (Bower and Reitman 1972).

The rhyming peg system has been proven to be an effective memory strategy for subjects of normal ability and subjects with learning disabilities (Elliot and Gentile 1986; Morris and Reid 1970). Some researchers have concluded that rhyming peg mnemonics may not be beneficial for elderly individuals (Mason and Smith 1977; Smith 1975; Hellebusch 1976), which may be due in part to their decreased visual imagery skills (Harris 1984). Patients with mild brain injuries appear to use this strategy more successfully than severely injured patients with more pronounced unilateral hemisphere damage (Wilson and Moffat 1984a).

The peg mnemonics and rhyming peg systems have been effective in teaching individuals lists of items as well as more complex concepts in school. For example, the peg system was used to teach high school students with learning disabilities about the hardness levels of minerals, colors and uses of minerals, and reasons for extinction of prehistoric reptiles in order of plausibility (Mastropieri, Scruggs, and Levin 1987). The peg system was found to be more effective than traditional instruction. The peg system has also been used to teach students to learn steps to complete a complex task. The students who used the peg system spent less time learning the steps and were able to remember more steps in correct order when completing the task (Timme et al. 1986).

PHONETIC MNEMONICS. Phonetic mnemonics is a rather complicated system consisting of assigning consonant sounds to the digits 0 to 9. The consonant sounds are combined with vowels to code numbers into words. Once the consonant-digit system is learned, numerical information can be coded into words, making it easier to remember. Key words can be generated using the consonant sounds. Once the key words are memorized, visual images are generated with other items to be remembered.

Minimal research has been conducted on the effectiveness of this system with patients who have memory difficulties. Patten (1972) used this strategy with patients who had severe verbal memory deficits and found that four of the seven subjects were able to use the strategy for remembering practical information. However, it took the subjects up to four weeks to learn the system. Research does indicate that subjects of normal ability find this strategy effective for remembering word lists, digits, and foreign language (Patton 1986; Gordon et al. 1984; Slak 1971; Paivio 1983).

This strategy is worth mentioning, given the above research; however, because of the complexity of the system, it does not appear to be very functional for individuals with memory impairments. For more information on this technique, refer to Higbee (1977b).

Remembering Names and Faces

A common complaint of older persons and individuals with memory impairment is that they are unable to recall people's names (Zelinski, Gilewski, and Thompson 1990; Wilson 1984). For individuals with memory deficits, visual imagery has been found to be an effective technique to learn and retain names (Moffat and Coward 1983). The mental image should be concrete; the simpler the better. For the name "Bill Applegate," an individual could visualize the person holding a dollar bill and an apple, walking through a gate. A picture could be drawn of this association and the patient could use the drawing in training to aid in recall of the name.

This strategy can be introduced in treatment by using fictitious names. Once the patient understands the concept of how the strategy works, it can then be used to learn therapists' names, new acquaintances, and so on.

Face-name association is a variation of this visualization strategy and involves making a visual association between the name and a distinctive feature of the person. For example, if Bill Applegate had red hair, the visualization could be of red apples sitting on his head with a gate around them.

Higbee (1988) suggests five steps to improve the ability to remember people's names.

- The first step is to make sure you hear the name. If someone is introducing a person, pay attention and listen to the name. Repeat the name several times, and spell the name out loud or to yourself.

- The next step is to make the name meaningful and concrete. Use substitute words for names that do not have any apparent meaning. For example, "man row" may be Monroe; "pole ant ski" may be Polanski.

- The third step is to focus on a distinctive feature of the person's face or appearance.

- Next, make a visual association between the name and the distinctive feature.

- The last step is to review the association and the person's name periodically.

These steps have been found to be effective with subjects who have normal memory skills and also with elderly subjects (Morris, Jones, and Hampson 1978; Yesavage, Rose, and Bower 1983). Individuals with brain damage find it much more difficult to use this strategy effectively on their own (Hill et al. 1987; Wilson 1987d).

Do not expect patients to learn too much at any one time, and be sure to follow a step-by-step sequenced program. As with all treatment, write out small, easily obtainable goals.

Motor Cuing

Motor cuing is a technique in which an action is associated with a person's name. The patient is asked to think of an action that symbolizes the name to be remembered. For example, "Pat" may be associated with the action of patting the knee. One patient with severe memory impairment was taught to recall the name "Anita" to the cue of shaking her hair (Wilson and Moffat 1984b). Anita was associated with "a neater way of doing her hair," paired with the person shaking her hair.

Jackson and Moffat (1983) taught an individual with severe memory impairment two lists of eight words using rehearsal and motor cue strategies. The patient recalled more words accurately using the motor cuing technique (mean recall using motor cuing technique = 7.58; mean recall using rehearsal technique = 3.17).

Rhyming

Rhyming is used to impose meaning on material to be remembered. A rhyme that incorporates the material to be learned will make the material more meaningful and easier to recall. A familiar rhyme that helps recall a spelling rule is, "i before e, except after c, or when sounded like a, as in neighbor or weigh." Another familiar rhyme is, "In fourteen hundred and ninety-two, Columbus sailed the ocean blue."

Organization

If an individual consciously organizes information to be learned, it is easier to retrieve. Categorizing information is an effective way to organize information. Research has shown that subjects are able to recall more words from a list if the words are categorized or grouped in some way (Baddeley and Warrington 1973). Children as young as 6 years of age were able to improve their memory of an 18-item list using the categorization strategy (Moely and Jeffrey 1974). Written paragraphs that are organized logically are also easier to recall than unorganized paragraphs (Myers, Pezdek, and Coulson 1973).

A study has also shown that visual information is recalled more efficiently if it is organized. Palmer (1975) found that coherent pictures where objects are organized in a meaningful way were easier to recall than objects in a jumbled picture. This gives support to the practice of keeping objects in the home in a well-organized manner, making it easier for patients to remember where to locate personal belongings.

Association

The association strategy refers to linking information to be learned with something that is already known. Learning builds on learning. Thinking of examples, comparing and contrasting, or rewording are all ways to associate what someone already knows with new information. Relating new ideas to information that is already known has proven to be an effective learning strategy (Reigeluth 1983).

One way to remember left from right is to look at one's hands. The left index finger and thumb form a capital "L" for "left." An easy way to remember the correct spelling of stationery is that "e" is for "envelope." The difference between stalactites and stalagmites is that stalactites grow from the ceiling and stalagmites grow from the ground. These are all examples of association strategies.

First-Letter Association

With first-letter mnemonics, an acronym or word is made out of the first letters of the items to be remembered. A similar technique can be used whereby a series of words or a phrase is formed from the first letters of the words to be remembered. This is called an acrostic. The following are examples of both acronyms and acrostics.

> *Acronym: ROY G. BIV* represents the colors of the rainbow: red, orange, yellow, green, blue, indigo, and violet.

> *Acrostic:* "A rat in the house might eat the ice cream" represents the word "arithmetic."

Research indicates that first-letter mnemonics is the most frequently used internal memory strategy (Harris 1980). It has also been proven to be effective with some individuals who have memory impairments as a result of brain damage (Wilson and Moffat 1984a).

Repetition and Relaxation

Repeating or rehearsing information helps to improve recall as long as it is used with other strategies. Continuing to study or rehearse after the information has been learned is called overlearning, which increases retrieval speed and strengthens learning (Wickelgren 1981). It also gives people more confidence that they know the material (Nelson et al. 1982).

Research suggests that anxiety can cause encoding, organization, and retrieval difficulties when taking examinations (Deffenbacher and Hazaleus 1985). Older individuals used mnemonic techniques more effectively after undergoing relaxation training (Yesavage 1984). Mental blocks occur most often when people are under stress. When a mental block occurs, it is best to take a break from trying to recall the item and come back to it later. The information may be easier to recall when the person is not trying so hard and is more relaxed (Reason and Lucas 1984).

Improving Recall of Written Information

There are several study skill strategies designed to improve recall of written information. Most are named by acronyms in which the letters represent the steps involved in using the system. Most of the systems are adaptations of one of the first systems developed, SQ3R.

SQ3R. The steps involved in the SQ3R system are as follows:

S: *Survey* the book, chapter, or article by reading the table of contents, chapter outline, summary, or discussion. Skim the written material and give particular attention to bold headings and pictures. This step is designed to give a general idea of what the written information is about.

Q: *Question.* Skim the reading material a second time, and think of five important questions about the text. Look for the answers to the questions as you are reading. This helps you focus on the reading material and gives a purpose for reading.

R: *Read* the written material in its entirety. Look for answers to your questions as you read.

R: *Recite.* Go over what you have read, stating the main points and details presented in the reading. Answer the questions you thought of in step 2. Write down key words or phrases as you summarize the reading.

R: *Review* what you have read. Look back for information in the reading that you cannot recall. Ask questions about the material again. Review the main points of what you just read. Review the information occasionally to refresh your memory. Remember that spaced reviews are better than continuous reviews.

Another reading strategy similar to SQ3R is the PQRST strategy (Robinson 1970). This acronym stands for preview, question, read, state, and test. Both the SQ3R and PQRST study strategies have been effective with individuals who have memory impairments due to brain damage (Glasgow et al. 1977; Grafman 1984; Wilson 1987c).

Comparing Internal Memory Strategies: Which One Is the Most Effective?

Wilson (1987a) compared several memory strategies for improving recall for subjects of normal ability and subjects with brain damage. The subjects were required to recall word lists using rehearsal, loci mnemonics, visual imagery, first-letter cuing, and storytelling strategies. The strategy found to be most useful for both groups was the storytelling technique, which required remembering items embedded in a story. Wilson suggested that the other strategies may have been more effective if the strategies were taught one step at a time and if shaping or chaining procedures were used.

Teaching Strategies

School plays an important role in preparing students with special needs to be successful at living and working as independently as possible. Clinicians may be called upon by classroom teachers to help these students develop memory and learning strategies. Teaching students strategies to compensate for their deficits is an important task. Clinicians may encounter high school and college students, and even working adults, who continue to seek help in developing strategies to cope with the increasing demands of life.

External Memory Aids

External memory aids are designed to store information externally and to cue individuals to take action. Memory books, grocery lists, computers, and maps are examples of external memory aids that store information. Cuing systems alert individuals that something needs to be done. Alarms, signs, and cue cards are examples of external memory aids that prompt individuals to complete a task or take action. (Appendix A lists external memory aids that are available commercially.)

Recent research has revealed that the use of external memory aids allows individuals to compensate successfully for their deficits. Batt and Lounsbury (1990) taught a 57-year-old male who had had a stroke a new skill of using a personal computer. Given his memory impairment, the client became frustrated with his inability to remember a previous computer command or decide what selection to make from the computer menu. An external memory aid in the form of a flow-chart system allowed the patient to learn to use the computer efficiently, decreased the patient's frustration when using the computer, aided in the development of self-esteem, and helped the patient to tolerate his disability.

In another research project, Wilson (1992) conducted a follow-up study of 25 clients with head injury who had received memory therapy five to ten years earlier. In 58% of the subjects, no changes in memory skills were measured by the Rivermead Behavioral Memory Test, which had been administered several years earlier; 31% of the subjects had improved memory test scores; and 11% received poorer scores. The most important finding was that a significant number of the clients were using more memory strategies and memory aids than before treatment or at the end of their rehabilitation program. This supports the theory that memory skills improve as a result of patients learning to compensate for their deficits.

Sohlberg and Mateer (1989) have described a training program for teaching individuals with severe memory impairment to use a memory book system independently to compensate for cognitive deficits. They have described how effective memory book use can be for improving skills needed for daily living and for employment.

Electronic memory aids have also been proven to be successful aids for individuals with brain damage. Giles and Shore (1989) have documented the effectiveness of a microcomputer system to improve functional skills. Teaching individuals to use written cue cards, written lists, and filing systems have been effective strategies to increase independence for individuals with brain injury (Milton 1985). Leng and Copello (1990) reviewed various approaches used in memory rehabilitation and found that external memory aids are useful for patients who have problems with remembering.

Among people with normal memory abilities, recent research indicates that certain age groups use different external memory aids because the memory tasks required of people change throughout the different stages of life (Petro et al. 1991). Research also suggests that the use of external memory aids is beneficial for older adults with memory impairments (Ciocon and Potter 1988).

4 Memory Training Programs

When Is Treatment Appropriate?

It is rare that the skills of individuals with brain damage return to premorbid levels with the passage of time or by playing memory games. This does not mean that their memory skills may not improve. But in most cases, residual memory deficits remain (Milner, Corkin, and Teuber 1968; Moffat 1984).

It is true that not all individuals will benefit from memory training or the use of internal or external memory strategies. For example, it is difficult for the clinician to have a functional impact on patients who deny they have memory deficits and therefore are not motivated to use the strategies taught in treatment. Each client is different in personality, type of memory problems, severity of memory deficits, and motivation to improve skills. Therefore, it is important to increase the patient's awareness of deficits, motivate the individual to try a variety of strategies, and determine which strategies work best for each particular client.

Memory training success is possible even a long time after injury. It is important for the clinician to realize that individuals with severe cognitive deficits learn very slowly and may require intensive, long-term treatment. Even small gains in memory skills can improve a patient's independence level, which is usually greatly appreciated by family members and caregivers.

Memory training is not appropriate for all clients. Clients in the final stages of degenerative diseases may no longer be able to benefit from treatment or even attend to environmental stimuli. Internal memory strategies are generally not as effective for individuals with primary degenerative diseases, and gains may be short-term due to the progressive nature of the disease. Focusing treatment on establishing external memory aid systems (labels, signs, daily schedule, and so forth) and training patient and family on external memory aid use tends to be more effective. Individuals with chemical and blood deficiencies or patients who are temporarily on medications that have side effects of reversible cognitive deficits may require only minimal treatment. Therapy should focus on educating the patient and family regarding the patient's deficits and safety precautions.

Developing Appropriate
Memory Training Programs

The memory strategies presented in this book have been used extensively with adolescents who have neurological impairments, and with adults who are experiencing memory difficulties. Teaching patients to compensate for their deficits by using internal and external memory aids has proven to be an effective way to increase their functional independence. Memory training programs have been established for patients in inpatient, outpatient, and home treatment settings.

It is important that all team members reinforce the use of memory strategies and follow a systematic training program. When a memory training program is being developed, the goal of treatment should be to teach the patient to compensate for deficits by using skills that are intact. Treatment activities should be functional and meaningful for the patient. If the patient does not believe in the treatment plan, chances are the individual will not generalize the strategies outside of treatment. The following suggestions may be helpful when establishing a memory training program.

- Establish a memory book system for yourself and consistently use the system. This will help you understand the importance of an individualized system, and you will be a good model for your patients.

- Train the interdisciplinary team members on the type of memory strategies that are appropriate for each patient. Encourage team members to reinforce the use of the strategies in their treatment sessions. The patient needs practice using the strategies in as many different settings and with as many different people as possible.

- Write specific, individualized behavioral objectives for each patient. Encourage the patient to assist in writing the objectives as part of your treatment, if possible. Have the patient file the objectives in the memory book. Review the objectives and progress made toward the objectives as part of your treatment session. All staff members involved with the patient should be trained on the patient's treatment program.

- The memory therapy exercises can be used in individual or group treatment settings. Group therapy can increase patients' awareness of their strengths and weaknesses.

- Involve family members and/or caregivers in treatment. Obtain information from family members regarding the patient's lifestyle, interests, previous learning styles, and strengths. This information should assist you in developing an individualized training program.

- If the patient denies having a memory impairment, ask the family to give examples of instances when the patient had difficulty remembering information and how it affects the person's independence. Be supportive in helping the patient understand these deficits, and reinforce the need to compensate to improve independence. Family members should be trained on the memory strategies being taught in treatment.

- Train family members and caregivers on how to use the memory book cuing hierarchy (see Cuing Hierarchy, p. 43) and how to reinforce the patient for memory book system use.

- Encourage the patient, family members, caregivers, team members, employers, and teachers to suggest additional memory book pages that could be included in the patient's memory book system. Incorporate additional pages in the patient's memory book as appropriate.

- Other professionals (certified psychologists, counselors, and others) can be helpful in assisting the patient in identifying the deficits and adjusting to the loss of skills. Be aware that depression may occur as the individual realizes the extent of the deficits, and that depression can impede the patient's ability to progress in treatment. All team members should work as an interdisciplinary team, providing consistent feedback to each other and to the patient regarding the patient's performance and behaviors.

Designing Individualized Programs

Each memory program should be designed to meet the individual's needs. Once you have determined the patient's needs and skill level, you can write treatment goals. You will need to work closely with the patient not only to determine the patient's ability to use specific strategies but also to determine the patient's activity preferences, interests, and motivation to learn strategies. If you develop a memory system that a patient is not interested in using or does not see the value of using, the patient will most likely not use the system outside the treatment setting.

Once the patient is able to demonstrate use of a strategy in structured treatment, attempt to incorporate the patient's interests or hobbies in treatment sessions. For example, if the patient enjoys cooking, design treatment activities around meal preparation. Require the patient to plan a meal, make a grocery list, purchase ingredients at the store, and prepare the meal. These are all functional activities which are excellent for training use of the memory book system and mnemonic strategies.

Observation of the patient completing functional activities such as these allows you to determine where difficulties in strategy use occur. You can then make necessary changes in the training program. Encourage patients to make suggestions for improving their memory systems. Involving patients in treatment planning can help motivate them to participate in treatment and to use their memory strategies.

Developing an External Memory Aid System

A memory book system should be designed individually for each patient. The patient's living environment, daily activities, and severity and type of memory impairment should be carefully considered when developing a memory book system. If possible, the patient, caregivers, and family members involved in the patient's care should participate in the development of the memory book system.

The reproducible Client Questionnaire can be of help in determining which memory book sheets should be included in the patient's memory book system. Family and caregiver input is most important to obtain a clear understanding of the patient's functional deficits. The patient may deny having memory deficits, so it is important to assess the patient's skills thoroughly using formal and informal test measures, clinical observations, and information obtained from family members and caregivers. Most often, the best information is obtained when observing the patient complete functional tasks in the therapy, home, and community environments.

Client Questionnaire

1. What problems have you experienced since your illness or injury?

    _____

    _____

    _____

2. Are you ever late to your scheduled appointments/classes? Why?

    _____

    _____

3. What do you like to do during your free time?

    _____

4. Do you do your own grocery shopping and meal preparation?

    _____

5. How do you remember what you need to buy when you go shopping?

    _____

6. Do you forget items you need to purchase when you go shopping?

    _____

7. Do you have difficulty recalling information about your injury/illness, such as when it occurred, how long you were in the hospital, and so forth?

    _____

8. Tell me about your past work history, educational background, and personal interests.

    _____

    _____

9. Do you ever have difficulty recalling information about work history, education, family history, or other facts?

    _____

10. What medications are you taking and why?

    _____

11. What means of transportation do you use?

_____

12. Do you ever ride the bus? How often?

_____

13. Do you ever have difficulty remembering which bus you need to take, or what time the bus arrives or departs?

_____

_____

14. Do you remember the names of your therapists? Who are they?

_____

_____

15. Do you use a technique or strategy for remembering peoples' names? What is it?

_____

_____

16. Are you responsible for paying your own monthly bills?

_____

17. Do you have difficulty remembering to pay bills and managing your monthly budget? What system do you use for paying bills?

_____

_____

18. Do you keep a list of important phone numbers, addresses, and birth dates? Where do you keep them?

_____

19. Do you ever have difficulty finding important phone numbers when you need them?

_____

20. What types of activities do you complete at home, school, or on the job?

_____

_____

21. Do you sometimes get distracted when you are trying to concentrate on something important? Do you have difficulty completing the project in a reasonable amount of time?

_____

_____

22. Do you sometimes forget verbal instructions that people give you? If yes, give an example.

_____

_____

_____

List examples of the type of memory difficulties you have experienced.

_____

_____

_____

What memory skills do you feel you need to improve?

_____

_____

_____

_____

Factors to Consider when Prescribing a Memory Book System

- *Type and severity of memory impairment:* A successful candidate needs to be able to remember information long enough to write it down on paper. The patient also needs to be able to follow a set procedure for recording and retrieving information.
- *Communication skills:* The patient needs to be able to process and follow single-step instructions and write legibly.
- *Physical limitations:* The patient needs to be able to manipulate the book well enough physically to locate pages efficiently.
- *Psychological adjustment:* The patient should have an awareness of the memory deficit, be motivated to compensate for the deficit, and be in a supportive environment.
- *Attention:* The patient needs to be able to attend to task for up to 5 minutes without verbal redirection.

Establishing and Training Memory Book Use

Develop the System

The first step in developing the memory book system is to determine the appropriate sections and pages to be included. Involve the patient, the patient's family, and clinicians who are familiar with the patient's skills. Keep the book simple at first, then include additional pages as the patient learns the system. Make sure each section of the book is clearly marked and easy to locate. Brightly colored notebook dividers with bold tabs are helpful for differentiating the sections of the book.

Teach the Memory Book Sections

The next step is to train the patient on the type of information that is to be recorded in each section of the book. (Appendix B contains some representative completed memory book pages as examples.) Rehearse how the sections are sequenced. Have the patient practice finding each section of the book and identifying the type of information that is to be recorded in each section. Ask the patient to visualize how the sections are sequenced in the book.

Simulated Practice Activities

Give the patient practice in recording and retrieving information in the book. Provide the patient with scenario worksheets of increasing complexity as the patient learns to use the system more effectively. (Practice worksheets are provided in Chapter Seven.)

Functional System Use

Create situations in and outside of therapy where the patient will be required to use the memory book system (example: ask the patient to schedule the next treatment appointment, ask the patient to bring something to the next treatment session, give the patient something important to remember, and so on).

Cue the patient to use the memory book system using the cuing hierarchy. Take the patient on outings in the community, and cue the patient to use the system as needed. Involve the patient's caregivers/family in the outings so they will become comfortable cuing the patient to use the system.

Memory Book Development: An Interdisciplinary Effort

All staff members working with the patient need to be involved in establishing the memory book system and using the system as part of treatment sessions. This may involve training staff members on the organization of the memory book system and how and when the system is to be used. Encourage other therapists to incorporate the patient's use of the memory book system into their treatment sessions. Suggest that they develop new pages that may be beneficial to the patient and increase independence. As a patient progresses in therapy, training sessions should expand out into the community where functional memory book training can take place.

Physicians and nurses should also be aware of the patient's memory book training program and encourage the patient to use the system to take notes regarding answers to medical questions, medication instructions, future appointments, and so forth. Some patients are more willing to take a physician's recommendation to use their memory book than clinicians' recommendations. Physician and medical staff support helps reinforce to the patient the importance of memory book use.

A written training program should be provided to all staff members working with the patient and to family members and caregivers. The treatment plan includes the rationale of the treatment program, treatment objectives, definitions, training procedure, and data collection. Give examples and role play appropriate cuing procedures with family and staff members who are unfamiliar with memory book training. Instruct staff members and caregivers on data collection procedures, and monitor the accuracy of data collection.

Suggested Memory Book Sequence

Reproducible memory book pages are included in Chapter 9 of this manual. The pages are set up to be used in a regular, hard-cover, three-ring binder. Use commercial notebook dividers to separate each section of the memory book. The patient's name label can be placed on the outside or inside cover for identification. Place the emergency information sheet in the inside cover of the notebook for easy access in case of an emergency. An enlarged emergency information sheet is provided for patients with visual impairments.

Note: The patient may not need all of the memory book sections included in this manual. Consider the patient's needs, and develop a system that is consistent with those needs. If the patient is easily confused by too many sections in the book, start by training the patient to use the schedule section, and gradually add sections as memory book training progresses.

A current monthly calendar should be the first page in the memory book. Blank calendars are provided in Chapter 9. The patient should be encouraged to write on the calendar appointments that are two or more weeks in the future. More immediate appointments would be placed on the daily schedule sheet. The patient should be cued to cross out each day on the calendar in order to quickly identify the current date.

Section 1: Daily Schedule

Several different schedule sheets are included in this manual. Determine which schedule is the easiest for the patient to use. You can determine this by completing several different schedules and asking the patient to accurately identify the date, treatment appointments, and activities on the daily "to do" list. The schedules which have a shaded box to the right of each time slot can help patients who have difficulty with temporal continuity. Instruct the patient to check the box as activities on the schedule are completed, to assist with orientation to time.

The daily schedule is designed to improve a patient's time management skills by listing all the activities the patient needs to complete for each day. This will help the patient remember scheduled appointments and plan for daily living and leisure activities. The schedule can also be used as a daily log. Encourage patients to write a brief note every 30 to 60 minutes about the activity they are engaged in, to improve recall of short-term information.

A weekly schedule is also included in this manual. This schedule usually works best with patients who have good vision, adequate time management skills, mild memory deficits, and good temporal orientation skills. The weekly schedule sheet is not designed to be used as a daily log. It is a good system for patients who need only to record important appointments or medication times.

Section 2: Reference

The reference section of the memory book is like an encyclopedia. Important information is organized in this section so that the patient can easily retrieve the information when needed. A blank table of contents sheet is provided. It is important that the client use the contents sheet in order to locate information efficiently in the memory book

Several other forms are provided. Use only the forms that are appropriate for your patient. Blank reference forms are also provided. The number of reference pages should increase as the patient continues to use the system. The patient may number the pages for quick reference. Pages appropriate for school-age patients are also provided.

PHONE NUMBERS AND ADDRESSES. Many patients already have a system for recording phone numbers, addresses, and important dates. However, patients using a memory book system find it easier to have all this information in one place for quick and easy reference. Blank address and phone number sheets are provided.

Section 3: Notes

Several blank note sheets are kept in this section for taking notes when needed. Encourage the patient to write all notes in this section instead of writing notes on loose paper and putting these in the notebook pockets. If the information is in the book, it is less likely to be misplaced or lost. The system needs to be structured and organized to make retrieval of information more efficient.

Information written in the Notes section of the book may need to be transferred to other sections of the book. For example, if the patient's physical therapist explains how to complete an exercise routine, the patient may need to write this information down in the Notes section of the book and later transfer the information to the Reference section.

Using Timers and Alarms

Some patients have difficulty using their memory book systems efficiently because they are unable to remember to look at the book to see what appointments they have scheduled. An alarm system can be used to remind the patient to look at the schedule. Some patients have difficulty remembering what the alarm is prompting them to do. A sign placed next to the alarm or on the watch can be effective in reminding the patient of the purpose of the alarm. Staff and family members should cue the patient to use the alarm in conjunction with the memory book. Nonspecific to specific cues should be given according to a written treatment plan.

Cuing Hierarchy

Clinicians, family members, and caregivers should follow the same cuing hierarchy when training a patient to use the memory book system. Attempt to keep the cues consistent across all trainers. Once the memory book system has been introduced and the patient demonstrates understanding of the system on simulated practice trials, begin functional training in real-life situations.

If a patient is given an appointment or something to do or remember, but the individual does not initiate memory book use, cue the patient using the following hierarchy:

Nonspecific cue: "This is something you will need to remember. What you do to help remind yourself?"

Specific cue: "You need to write that in your memory book because that is something you will need to remember. In what section of your book should you write that?"

Gestural cue: Open the patient's book to the appropriate section and explain why the information should be placed here. Point to the appropriate place in the patient's book where the information should be written.

Model: Write the information in the appropriate section of the patient's book. Ask the patient to read what you have written, and have the person explain why the information belongs in that section of the memory book.

When training staff or caregivers on using a cuing hierarchy, be sure to stress that the patient should be given every opportunity to initiate memory book use with the fewest cues possible. Therefore, it is important to give the patient time to process the cue and to respond. The individual providing the cue needs to be careful not to provide more cues than necessary or to provide additional cues prematurely. A 15-second interval between cues is a good guideline. Some patients may require more time to process the cue and initiate memory book use. The cuing procedure should be clearly stated on the patient's written behavioral plan.

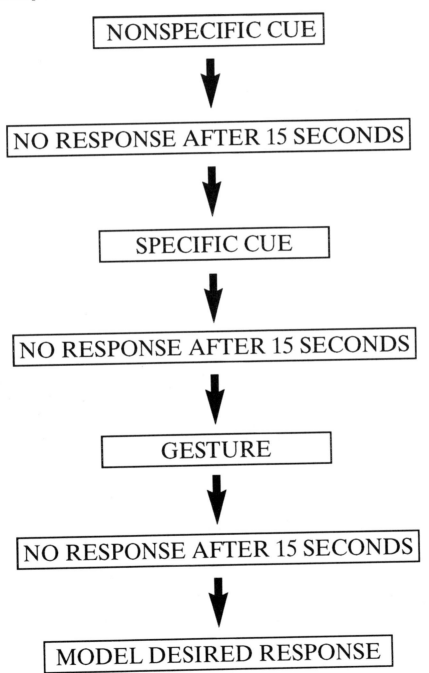

NONSPECIFIC CUE

↓

NO RESPONSE AFTER 15 SECONDS

↓

SPECIFIC CUE

↓

NO RESPONSE AFTER 15 SECONDS

↓

GESTURE

↓

NO RESPONSE AFTER 15 SECONDS

↓

MODEL DESIRED RESPONSE

A variety of specific and nonspecific cues can be given. There is a continuum of specificity within the nonspecific and specific cue types. A nonspecific cue can be very general or it can be more direct or specific. For example, both of the following are considered nonspecific cues: "That is important information"; "That is important information that you need to remember." Both of these are non-specific cues because the patient is not being told to write the information in the memory book. However, the second cue is more specific or direct than the first.

As the patient progresses with training memory book use, change the cues you provide. If a patient experiences difficulty in one phase of the cuing hierarchy (for example, the person consistently requires a nonspecific cue), adjust the cue so that it is less and less direct until the individual does not require any cuing.

Frequency of Training

The frequency and duration of treatment sessions will vary from patient to patient, depending on the severity of impairment. Generally, patients with severe impairments require more frequent training sessions and a longer duration of treatment. Some patients with severe impairment have difficulty remembering previous training sessions or that they have a memory book system in place. In these cases, it is important to use visual and auditory cues (signs, pagers, alarms) in the environment to remind the patient to use the system.

With patients who have severe difficulties, caregivers and family members may become the primary trainers of the system because they spend the most time with the patient, and training needs to occur frequently during each day. With all patients, it is important that memory book training occur in all treatment sessions and that caregivers continue to reinforce system use throughout the day.

Family Support

Support by family members and caregivers is key to memory training success in most cases. Family members and caregivers should have a clear understanding of each memory strategy and how it is used. Encourage them to remind the patient that the goal of training is to increase independence, and to cue the patient appropriately to use the strategies throughout the day.

Generalization

Throughout this book, it has been stressed that training should occur in a variety of settings and with a variety of people. The wider the range of settings in training, the more likely the strategy will generalize to other settings (Carr 1980). Patients must learn to generalize the skills learned in therapy across settings and behaviors in order to be independent and functional with memory book use. The memory book training program should account for generalization across settings. That is why it is important that caregivers and family members be trained in cuing the patient to use the memory book outside the structured therapy setting. As functional opportunities arise to use the memory book system, the patient should be reinforced to use the skills that have been taught in therapy settings.

Data Collection

Consistent, accurate data should be kept on the patient's performance at all levels of memory book training. On structured treatment activities, encourage patients to predict their accuracy on practice tasks and to keep data on their accuracy. Summarize the data at the end of the session and compare performance to previous sessions. The patient can keep data graphs or cards in the front of the memory book, to track the progress being made each session.

Some patients experience specific problems in memory book training. They may forget to bring their books to treatment or to update their daily schedules. This behavior should be targeted and data collected each session.

Keeping Data on Carryover Activities

Each patient should be observed using the memory book system in a variety of environments outside the structured therapy room. To measure a patient's progress toward independent use of the memory book system, keep data on the amount of cuing needed to record information successfully in the memory book system.

The following data sheets can be used by all team members and caregivers working with a patient. As team members give the patient important information to remember, they record the amount of cuing required for the patient to write the information accurately in the memory book. When information is requested of the patient, the patient's ability to access the information in the memory book is recorded. Keep data on the patient's ability to record and retrieve information in individual and group settings. It is also important to measure the patient's ability to use the memory book system spontaneously without cues outside of treatment, in the living environment.

Patient Data Record Sheet

Patient:

Date:

Activity/Class:

Non-Specific Cue To Be Given:

Specific Cue To Be Given:

		Recording Information	
		Retrieving Information	

Cue Provided:			Comments:
		No Cue Required	
		Non-Specific Cue	
		Specific Cue	
		Gestural Cue	
		Model	
		Refusal	

		Recording Information	
		Retrieving Information	

Cue Provided:			Comments:
		No Cue Required	
		Non-Specific Cue	
		Specific Cue	
		Gestural Cue	
		Model	
		Refusal	

		Recording Information	
		Retrieving Information	

Cue Provided:			Comments:
		No Cue Required	
		Non-Specific Cue	
		Specific Cue	
		Gestural Cue	
		Model	
		Refusal	

		Recording Information	
		Retrieving Information	

Cue Provided:			Comments:
		No Cue Required	
		Non-Specific Cue	
		Specific Cue	
		Gestural Cue	
		Model	
		Refusal	

Group Data Sheet

Cue Provided	Patient:	Recording Information
No Cue Required	Class / Activity:	
Non-specific Cue		
Specific Cue		Retrieving Information
Gestural Cue		
Model		
Refusal		

Cue Provided	Patient:	Recording Information
No Cue Required	Class / Activity:	
Non-specific Cue		
Specific Cue		Retrieving Information
Gestural Cue		
Model		
Refusal		

Cue Provided	Patient:	Recording Information
No Cue Required	Class / Activity:	
Non-specific Cue		
Specific Cue		Retrieving Information
Gestural Cue		
Model		
Refusal		

Cue Provided	Patient:	Recording Information
No Cue Required	Class / Activity:	
Non-specific Cue		
Specific Cue		Retrieving Information
Gestural Cue		
Model		
Refusal		

Cue Provided	Patient:	Recording Information
No Cue Required	Class / Activity:	
Non-specific Cue		
Specific Cue		Retrieving Information
Gestural Cue		
Model		
Refusal		

Training Programs for Patients with Severe Impairments

Some patients are unable to learn to use memory book systems and internal memory strategies due to the severity of their impairments and related cognitive deficits. Keep in mind that individuals with memory impairment require a great deal of repeated practice before learning to use the system. However, some patients do not progress toward independent system use, and other patients may be unable to use a memory book system because of language or physical impairments.

These patients may benefit from less complicated systems that rely less on procedural memory, reasoning, and organization skills. A large dry-erase board can be used to write the daily schedule and reminders of things to do. If the patient is unable to read, pictures can be used on the schedule to represent times and activities. Establish a bulletin board with pictures of family members, pets and friends, and personal information. Visual cues such as written signs or icons placed in the environment can also be helpful reminders. (See the section on Alternatives to Memory Book Systems in this chapter.)

Patients with severe impairments generally require increased training time to learn information adequately. Family and caregivers may be required to provide training of system use depending on available resources. Provide a systematic written training program for the family and caregivers to follow. Review the program data periodically to determine the program's effectiveness.

Depending on the etiology of the cognitive disorder, return of cognitive functioning may occur over time. As the patient's memory skills improve, most often there is an improvement in attention and other cognitive skills. The patient can progress to a more complicated, efficient memory system, such as a memory book, as skills improve.

It is difficult to determine which patients will be successful in using specific memory strategies. Cognitive test scores do not always indicate whether a patient will be successful at memory book training. There are many factors involved in memory book training in addition to the severity of the cognitive impairment. In many cases, a rehabilitation team will indicate that, based on test results, the prognosis for independent use of a memory book system is poor. However, with consistent training and family support, the patient is able to use the memory book system to overcome barriers which have kept the patient from living and working independently. The patient's formal cognitive test scores remain unchanged, but the patient is able to compensate for cognitive deficits using a memory book system.

Be flexible when training memory book system use. If the system is too complicated and the patient demonstrates little or no ability to learn to use the system, develop a simpler alternative system, so the patient is able to demonstrate success.

Alternatives to Memory Book Systems

Patients who are unable to learn to use a memory book system because of the severity of their cognitive deficits may become frustrated with their attempts to use the system independently. It may be necessary to abandon a memory book training program if a patient is unable to progress toward the objectives or becomes frustrated or distressed with the training program. Clinicians must observe the training process closely and determine when to abandon one strategy and begin training on another.

Schedule Boards

If memory book training is unsuccessful, other external memory aids such as activity or schedule boards may be more appropriate. These boards consist of enlarged daily, weekly, or monthly calendars in which appointments and activities can easily be added or removed. Use picture icons to represent activities and appointments for patients who are unable to read. Laminate icons and photographs representing appointments, activities, and times of day, and attach hook-and-pile tape to fasten these on the boards. Emergency phone numbers, "to do" lists, and personal information can be incorporated into these boards according to the patient's needs. Establish a systematic training procedure for training any memory system use.

Electronic Day Planners

There are numerous electronic day planners currently on the market. Most of these systems are complicated to use and require good visual and procedural memory skills. Many of the systems have programmable alarm systems built into the units. The alarm can be programmed to sound prior to scheduled appointments. Some of these systems may be appropriate for patients who are functioning at higher levels. (See Appendix A for a listing of electronic organizers.)

5 Sample Behavioral Plans and Case Studies

Determining barriers to independence and developing a treatment plan to eliminate those barriers are two important steps in establishing a memory training program. This chapter includes examples of how to develop a problem list and write treatment goals and objectives. Sample treatment plans and case studies are also provided to assist you in establishing effective memory training programs for your clients.

Developing a Problem List

The goal of treatment should be to improve the patient's functional independence or to improve the individual's ability to complete daily activities with less assistance and more efficiency. Problems that affect daily activities should be determined by observation, patient interview, family and caregiver interview, interviews with employers or teachers, and consultation with other clinicians or care providers.

Once a problem list has been established, it is important that the patient and family assist in prioritizing the problems. Rank the items, from the problem that most negatively affects the patient's level of independence to the problem that least negatively affects independence. Prioritizing the problems often helps motivate patients to learn and use strategies, because it helps clients see the importance of the activity in light of how it impacts their lives.

For example, the following problems were noted and prioritized for a 19-year-old patient with a closed head injury and mild memory deficits:

1. unable to find classrooms on community college campus
2. difficulty remembering class assignments
3. difficulty remembering details presented in textbook
4. difficulty remembering details during classroom lectures
5. difficulty completing class projects on time
6. difficulty organizing finances

Another patient was a 59-year-old man who had had a right CVA and lived in a retirement community. His six most important problems were prioritized as follows:

1. difficulty remembering to turn off appliances such as the stove and iron, and to turn down furnace when leaving his apartment

2. inability to remember biographical information such as his address, phone number, and date of birth

3. difficulty remembering to take medications

4. difficulty remembering appointments

5. difficulty remembering names of less familiar family members and clinicians

6. inability to complete projects around the house (pay bills, get groceries, run errands, and so on)

Each of these patients had very different problem lists based on their lifestyles and the type and severity of impairment.

Writing Goals and Objectives

Once a problem list is established, you will write behavioral objectives. Writing behavioral objectives allows you and the patient to know the precise goal of treatment and when the goal has been achieved. Behavioral objectives allow patients to know what they are supposed to be doing, what is to be accomplished, and under what conditions. It also provides a framework for you to measure the success of the training. When progress is measurable, it is easy for the patient to observe progress. Visually representing the patient's responses on a graph or data sheet can be very motivating for you and the patient.

Consider the problem of difficulty remembering appointments. The first step is to gather data on the ratio of forgetting to remembering appointments. For example, one patient had an average of eight therapy appointments scheduled during the week, and the appointment times changed from week to week. The patient remembered two of the eight scheduled appointments without any cuing during the first week. The patient wrote his appointments on his calendar but did not remember to look on his calendar systematically.

The following training goal was established: Patient will attend 100% of all scheduled appointments for two consecutive weeks. A set of small, systematic objectives or steps was written and worked on each session.

- A daily schedule section will be established in the patient's memory book.

- The patient will demonstrate the ability to write scheduled appointments accurately in his memory book on four out of four opportunities with no cues.

- The patient will accurately set his wrist timer each morning to ring every 30 minutes on five consecutive days.
- The patient will check the daily schedule section of his memory book every 30 minutes.

Several strategies were used to assist the patient in obtaining his goal. The patient participated in making choices in treatment which gave him a greater sense of control over therapy. For example, several memory book systems and schedule types were presented to the patient that were appropriate for his level of functioning. The pros and cons of each system were discussed, and the patient chose the system he preferred. Given that the patient walked to his therapy appointments, he chose a smaller system because it was easy to carry.

The patient learned to copy appointments in his memory book accurately after several trials. Photocopies of his schedule section were made, and he did a number of practice exercises. The patient was required to record a number of appointments in his book from appointment cards, similar to the ones he received from his therapists and doctors. Each of the therapists who worked with this patient kept data on how accurately he recorded his next therapy appointment in his memory book. The patient kept a data sheet inside the cover of his book on which each therapist marked whether the task was completed accurately or if he required cues. During the first week of training, the client did not attend to the date on the schedule and frequently recorded his appointment on the following day's schedule. Error frequency decreased with consistent feedback from his therapists.

A written sign was placed on the patient's bathroom mirror to remind him to set and put on his wrist timer. Initially, the patient required written cues for setting the wrist timer. With practice, the patient was able to use the cue sheet less and less until eventually he was able to discard the cue sheet.

This patient originally had difficulty remembering what he was to do when his wrist watch alarm sounded, which was to look at the schedule section of his memory book. Therapists and rehabilitation aides were trained on a cuing hierarchy to increase the patient's success on this objective. The cuing hierarchy was as follows:

Nonspecific cue: "The alarm is to remind you to do something. What are you supposed to do when the alarm sounds?"

Specific cue: "You are to look in your memory book. Which section of your book are you to look at?"

Additional cue: "You are to look at your daily schedule to see what appointment you have scheduled next."

Visual cue: Aide turns to daily schedule and points to next appointment.

The aides and therapists kept data on how much cuing was required before the patient looked at the appropriate section of his book to locate what he had scheduled next. This patient progressed rapidly, and within three weeks he was using his alarm and daily schedule section of his book independently.

It is important to be systematic in training. Providing consistent feedback to the patient regarding performance, and providing a number of opportunities for the patient to practice the skill in a variety of settings with a variety of people, are important factors in memory book training. Staff training is key to a successful treatment program. Provide written programs for all family and staff members involved in training. The written program should state the patient's goal, intervention strategies, specific cues to be provided, and feedback to be given. Keep data collection simple, and encourage everyone to record data in the same manner. Check that all family members and staff are recording data and cuing the patient correctly and consistently.

Sample Treatment Plans

The following sample treatment plans can be used as guides when writing individualized treatment plans for patients. Treatment plans should be detailed, providing enough specific information so that any trained clinician or family member could implement the program with little or no assistance. The treatment plan should include the rationale for the program, the objective(s) of the program, definitions of terms used in the program description, and instructions on how to collect and record data.

Sample Treatment Plan 1: Schedule Board Use

One patient was unsuccessful at using a memory book system because of poor procedural memory and organization skills. When unsupervised, this patient removed the pages from her memory book and became frustrated with her inability to put them back into the system in the correct order. The book was more frustrating than beneficial for this patient. The clinicians and the patient worked together in establishing a schedule board system that required less organizational and procedural memory skills than the memory book system. (See Alternatives to Memory Book Systems in Chapter 4.)

Rationale
The patient has difficulty keeping track of appointments and scheduled activities secondary to short-term and organizational difficulties. She has a calendar but has not been able to use it independently since her injury. A schedule board system has been established. This program is designed to develop independent use of this memory/time management device.

Objective
Make no scheduling errors for one month.

Definitions

Spontaneously: from memory without cues

Spontaneously, referring to schedule board: independently initiating check of calendar for information with cues

Scheduling error: missing appointment or being unprepared for scheduled event because of inaccurately recording date or time of event/appointment or because of failing to record event/appointment at all

Cuing Hierarchy

1. No cue required: patient *independently* answers or spontaneously uses calendar.

2. Nonspecific cue: a general cue given to remind the patient to remember an event (example: "This is something important to remember").

3. Specific cue: stating specifically that something should be written on the calendar to remember it (example: "You should write this on your calendar so that you can remember it").

4. Gestural cue: pointing exactly to where the information should be written on the schedule and repeating the specific cue.

5. Model: writing the information on the schedule board. Ask the patient to read what you have written.

Procedure: Prompting when Recording Scheduled Event/Appointment

Go through the steps below whenever the patient should record an activity that occurs on a specific day at a specific time.

1. Watch the patient as she records information. If the patient does not initiate recording appointments or scheduled events, go through the cuing hierarchy described earlier.

2. Observe whether she checks what she has written for accuracy (that is, written on correct date with correct information regarding time and event). If she does not, cue her to do so using the above hierarchy.

3. If she fails to locate an error after self-checking, cue her again to correct the error using the same cuing hierarchy.

Data Collection

Record data on the patient's data record sheet.

Sample Treatment Plan 2:
Information and Time Management Program

Rationale

This patient currently relies on others to manage his time. Additionally, he requires checklists and written cues to help him complete tasks. Use of a memory notebook with sections for a daily schedule, checklists, things to do, and things to remember would increase his independence. This program is designed to train the patient to utilize a memory book system.

Objectives

- The patient will identify all sections of his memory book on three consecutive sessions.
- The patient will turn to the appropriate section of his memory book to obtain requested information with 90% or greater accuracy on three consecutive trials.
- The patient will write or accurately copy all appointments onto his daily schedule for two consecutive weeks.
- The patient will state month, day, date, and year accurately on five consecutive days.

Definitions

Memory book sections will include but not be limited to:

- monthly calendar
- daily schedule
- "to do" list
- reference
- telephone numbers/addresses

Procedure

Each day a therapist or the caregiver will review the patient's calendar, daily schedule, and "to do" list (including therapy appointments, outside appointments, recreation plans, chores, and others). Any appointments that are not on the calendar and daily schedule should be added.

Ask the patient to check his schedule when he completes an activity so he will know what to do next. Provide cuing along a hierarchy from nonspecific to specific until the patient is able to locate the needed information.

During the day, have the patient refer to his memory book to locate information he needs as opportunities arise.

When the patient achieves the above objective, establish additional objectives that target independent use of his memory book.

Data Collection

Record patient's responses on data sheet. Data will be graphed weekly by the clinicians.

Case Studies

Case Study #1

This 66-year-old male had experienced a right CVA. He was admitted to the hospital after presenting with weakness and incoordination in his left upper extremity and left facial weakness. A head CT scan showed right basal ganglia and right posterior parietal white matter hypodensities. Medical reports indicated that when the patient was admitted to the hospital, he was oriented to name and physical deficits, but not to day of the week, date, and year.

The patient exhibited perseveration, significant left neglect and visual perceptual deficits, decreased mental flexibility, decreased attention and concentration, and mild to moderate memory deficits. Speech and language skills were intact. The patient participated in a three-week inpatient therapy program where he received physical therapy, occupational therapy, speech therapy, counseling, and nursing services. The patient's left neglect, as well as his other cognitive deficits, decreased during inpatient treatment.

After inpatient treatment, the patient returned home to live with family members in a separate living area of the house. The patient required assistance from his family to remind him to make his meals, take his medications, and complete other daily living tasks. As reported by his family, the patient appeared to lack the ability to initiate and follow through on these tasks. The patient's family checked on him every hour to provide assistance if needed.

The patient received speech and occupational therapy services at home. The goal of treatment was to increase functional independence at home and to decrease the amount of supervision and assistance required of the family. The family was able to provide long-term assistance in the morning and evening hours but wanted to be able to leave the patient alone during the day without supervision.

Formal and informal tests were administered to assess the patient's cognitive and visual-perceptual skills. Test results revealed adequate reasoning and judgment skills for daily living needs. The patient occasionally required cues to locate left margin when reading or completing a form. The patient experienced difficulty following verbal instructions that were greater than two steps when completing a task. He experienced difficulty answering content questions regarding short stories, especially after a 15-minute delay. Decreased organization and attention skills were noted during a simulated checkbook task. The patient was unable to recall a four-item errand list after a 15-minute delay.

The patient's major complaints were that he was unable to remember information people told him and that he did not enjoy reading because he was unable to remember details of what he read. The patient presented with mild temporal orientation deficits. Prior to his injury, the patient did not socialize outside his family, and he described himself as a "loner."

Through observation of the patient in his home environment and consultation with the patient and the patient's family, a list of problem areas was developed. The list consisted of difficulties the patient exhibited that negatively affected his functional independence. The patient was retired. Prior to his stroke, he had spent most of his leisure time reading. The family and patient came to agreement on the ranking of this list from most to least problematic. The problem list was as follows:

- difficulty remembering to take medications
- difficulty organizing bills, paying bills on time, and managing his checkbook
- difficulty remembering appointments and poor follow-through on a variety of daily activities, including preparing and eating meals
- difficulty attending to leisure reading material and remembering details of what he read

Cognitive Training Program

This patient was seen three days a week for eight weeks. Treatment sessions lasted 60 minutes. The patient's daughter and son-in-law were present during training sessions and participated as appropriate. A 15-minute family consultation occurred after each treatment session. Co-treatment with the occupational therapist was conducted during one session every other week. Additionally, a 30-minute consultation session with the patient's occupational therapist occurred weekly.

Obtaining Baseline Data

MEDICATION SCHEDULE. Baseline was taken on the patient's ability to take his medication for three consecutive days. The patient was required to take his medications three times a day, with breakfast, lunch, and dinner. Once a week, a family member filled a pill organizer that was clearly marked with the days of the week and the times of day the pills were to be taken.

A baseline data sheet was developed, and the patient's daughter was trained on taking data on the patient's ability to remember to take his medications without cues. The patient's medication organizer was checked one-half hour after each meal was completed. The patient's daughter then recorded whether the patient took his medication independently or required prompting to do so. The patient required prompting on seven of the nine baseline trials.

CHECKBOOK MANAGEMENT. A simulated checkbook task was developed for training and was used to obtain baseline data. Actual copies of the patient's checkbook ledger, checks, and bills were used to make the task as functional as possible. Data was taken on three steps: writing the checks accurately, recording the check amounts accurately on the ledger, and accurately calculating the checking account balance. The patient was given five bills to pay on three consecutive sessions to establish baseline data. Results are as follows:

Trial Session 1

Wrote check accurately 2/5
Recorded amount accurately on ledger 4/5
Accurately calculated checking account balance 3/5

Trial Session 2

Wrote check accurately 3/5
Recorded amount accurately on ledger 3/5
Accurately calculated checking account balance 4/5

Trial Session 3

Wrote check accurately 3/5
Recorded amount accurately on ledger 5/5
Accurately calculated checking account balance 2/5

Total Accuracy on Three Trials

Wrote check accurately 8/15 (53%)
Recorded amount accurately on ledger 12/15 (80%)
Accurately calculated checking account balance 9/15 (60%)

TIME MANAGEMENT. The patient's daughter posted a hand-written schedule on the patient's kitchen table each day to remind the patient to make his meals, take a shower, complete his exercise routine, and so forth. The schedule was fairly consistent from day to day. The family reported that the patient rarely remembered to look at the schedule and frequently threw the schedule away when cleaning up his living area. The patient's daughter, occupational therapist, and speech therapist took data for three consecutive days. If the patient initiated the scheduled task within one-half hour of the scheduled time, he received credit for task completion. If the patient did not initiate the task, he was prompted to initiate the task and the prompt was recorded. Baseline data was as follows:

Day One

Number of tasks to complete 6
Number of prompts required 5
Follow-through after prompt 5/5

Day Two

Number of tasks to complete 6
Number of prompts required 4
Follow-through after prompt 4/4

Day Three

Number of tasks to complete 7
Number of prompts required 6
Follow-through after prompt 6/6
Total tasks to complete over three days 19
Total number of prompts required 15
Follow-through after prompt 15/15 (100%)

READING COMPREHENSION. Reading comprehension baseline data was taken on the patient's ability to recall details on three four- to five-page short stories. The patient read a short story and, after a 15-minute delay, answered ten questions about the content of the story. All questions required one- or two-word answers. On three consecutive sessions, the patient scored 4/10, 5/10, and 4/10, respectively.

Training of Time Management and Medication Schedule

A memory book system was established which consisted of a daily schedule, a list of things to remember, and a telephone message section. The patient and family chose the type of schedule and pages for the "things to remember" section which were appropriate for the patient's lifestyle and needs. The patient and family appeared motivated to use the system and provided input for the patient's written treatment goals. A goal sheet and data form for each goal were placed in the patient's memory book. A written program for each goal was reviewed with the patient's family. The treatment goals were as follows:

1. The patient will take his medication independently at scheduled times with no cues from family members on five consecutive days.

2. The patient will accurately write checks and balance check ledger given bill statements on five consecutive trials

3. The patient will complete all activities on his schedule for five consecutive days.

4. The patient will answer content questions about four- to five-page stories after a 15-minute delay with 90% accuracy.

Goal #1 was actually included in goal #3 because the patient's medication schedule was on his daily schedule. However, the patient and the family wanted a separate goal for taking medication because they felt that more importance needed to be placed on meeting this goal.

Small, sequenced objectives were established for each training session, and these were reviewed with the patient and his family. The majority of the time spent in treatment focused on training the family on the treatment programs, cuing hierarchies, and data collection procedures. Family members were easily trained, and their follow-through on the treatment program was excellent.

This patient's memory book system was established with the objective of meeting all of his treatment goals. The daily schedule section reminded the patient to take his medications, pay his bills, manage his time efficiently, and remember his appointments and daily living activities. His "things to remember" section had a written list of steps to follow to improve recall of written stories. An alarm system was established, and it sounded every 30 minutes. A written sign was placed next to the alarm that said, "Look in your memory book." When the alarm sounded, the patient saw the sign, looked at the schedule in his book, then completed the activity scheduled at that time. The patient's daughter stayed with the patient in his living area during the first four weeks of training to provide consistent cues and feedback.

The memory book training was presented in three phases. The first phase consisted of teaching the basic function of the system: reviewing the pages in the book, what information belonged in each section, and how the book was organized. The second phase of training involved structured practice assignments, which included recording and retrieving information in the book to increase efficiency of the system use. The last phase involved using the system in the patient's environment to improve functional independence.

These phases were similar for teaching recall of details in written stories. The SQ3R reading method was used to help this patient meet his reading comprehension goal. The patient was first taught the procedure of how to use the system. (The patient made a written checklist of the procedure and placed it in his memory book.) The second phase consisted of structured practice using the strategy on stories provided by the clinician. Once the patient was able to use the strategy in therapy, he was then required to use the strategy outside of treatment when reading for leisure.

This patient met all of his goals in eight weeks and was able to stay at home alone without assistance during the day. Telephone interviews with the patient's daughter were conducted 3, 6, 12, and 24 weeks post discharge from therapy. The results of the interview questionnaire indicated that up to six months after discharge, the patient continued to use his memory book system and was able to complete daily living activities and take his medications as scheduled. The patient's daughter continued to assist the patient each morning in completing the schedule for the day and indicated that she enjoyed this task. The patient continued to use an alarm to remind him to look at his book and to follow his schedule. The patient's daughter reported that the patient used the memory book system as well or better at six months post discharge from treatment compared to how efficiently he used the system at the time of discharge. Reportedly, the patient was referring to and recording more information in the "things to remember" section of his book six months after discharge.

The patient's daughter reported a decrease in the patient's use of the SQ3R reading strategy 6 weeks post discharge. At 24 weeks post discharge, it was reported that the patient used the SQ3R strategy only occasionally. However, the patient's daughter did report that the patient continued to read for pleasure each day and appeared to retain the information he read. The patient's reading comprehension and recall may have improved over time, or he may have internalized the strategy and no longer needed to follow the program steps.

There were several factors that were important to the success of the memory book training program with this case:

- The patient was aware of his deficit areas.
- The patient was motivated to use an external memory strategy.
- The family was supportive and consistent in training system use.
- The family was motivated to increase the patient's independence level.

Case Study #2

This 19-year-old male had been involved in a motor vehicle accident and had sustained a closed head injury, following which he was unconscious for 30 minutes. A head CT scan showed no abnormalities. The patient was hospitalized for 48 hours and then released. Two months post injury, the patient was referred by his physician for outpatient speech pathology. The patient had been attending a community college at the time of the accident. After the accident, he complained of decreased performance at school, specifically decreased ability to concentrate on school tasks and to recall information presented verbally or in writing. The patient was a 4.0 student prior to the motor vehicle accident.

Formal testing revealed below-average ability to follow oral directions. The patient presented with no speech disorders; word finding skills were intact. Reading comprehension skills on formal test measures were in the average range. The patient read a high-school-level textbook chapter and answered content questions with 90% accuracy with no delay, and with 50% accuracy following a 30-minute delay. No perceptual problems were observed. The patient was able to recall details from a 5-minute lecture with 100% accuracy with no delay, and with 70% accuracy after a 30-minute delay. The patient demonstrated good organization in his writing and appeared to have good study habits.

The test results were reviewed with the patient, and the following problem areas were identified as most negatively affecting the patient's performance at school:

- difficulty remembering detailed information presented verbally with a delay
- difficulty remembering detailed written information with a delay

Cognitive Training Program

This patient was seen two days a week for three weeks. Treatment sessions lasted 60 minutes. A memory book system was established to provide a structured system for the patient to take notes and to track assignments, projects, and test dates. The patient was trained to use mnemonic strategies to assist in recall of written and verbal information. The patient's school notes and textbook reading material were used as stimuli for mnemonic training. Treatment goals were as follows:

1. The patient will identify and adequately demonstrate use of three mnemonic strategies for memorizing lists of information.

2. The patient will read a textbook chapter and answer content questions with 90% accuracy after a 30-minute delay.

3. The patient will write appointments and other information to remember (including class assignments and test schedule) in the appropriate sections of his memory book with at least 90% accuracy for three consecutive weeks.

SESSION #1

Mnemonic strategies. This patient reported that he used only rehearsal when studying for examinations. Examples of storytelling, first-letter cue, categorization, and loci mnemonics were presented during the first treatment session. The patient completed worksheets, practicing the strategies.

The recall of information on these structured tasks was excellent, even after a 30-minute delay (90% to 100% for 12-item lists). A written handout on the mnemonic strategies taught during this session was provided for the patient to review prior to the next session. The patient was instructed to use the strategies in class if possible and to record the type of strategies he used on his schedule in his memory book.

Memory book. After reviewing several memory book examples, the patient determined that a system consisting of four sections would be most appropriate for him at school and at home. The sections consisted of a daily schedule, things to do, things to remember, and class notes. A blank note pad section was added for the patient to take notes if someone were to give lengthy verbal instructions. Given scenarios, the patient accurately identified the appropriate section of his book in which to place the information on 19 out of 20 trials. The patient appeared to have a good understanding of how to use his system. He developed a cue sheet to remind him of the type of information that was to be recorded in each section for future reference.

SESSION #2

Mnemonics. The patient brought classroom reading material and class notes to the second treatment session. The patient met goal #1 during this session by adequately demonstrating the use of first-letter cue, storytelling, and categorization strategies using information from his classroom notes. The schedule section of his memory book was reviewed to assess which mnemonic strategies the patient was using in class and study activities. The patient used categorization and first-letter cue strategies most often, and he reported that he preferred using these strategies.

The patient brought a handout to the session that he had received from one of his classes, listing the names of 32 engine parts he needed to remember. The patient divided the engine into four subsections and categorized the parts on his list. He then developed a first-letter cue system to assist in remembering the parts in each category. The patient rehearsed his list, writing down the mnemonic cues as he practiced. After a 30-minute delay, the patient was able to recall 31 of the 32 engine parts with no cues.

Memory book. The patient was able to recall all the sections of his book with no cues and give two appropriate examples of the type of information to be recorded in each section. The patient's memory book entries were reviewed. Daily schedule entries appeared accurate, and the patient appeared to be using the sections of his book appropriately. He reported one recording error in which he wrote an appointment on the incorrect day. The patient was responsible for keeping data on the errors he made when recording information in his memory book.

The patient accurately recorded his next treatment appointment in his memory book spontaneously. He also noted on his daily schedule what was worked on in treatment during this session.

Reading comprehension. The patient was introduced to the SQ3R reading strategy. The patient reported that his reading strategy was to reread textbook chapters several times prior to taking an examination and occasionally highlight main points in the chapter. A worksheet outlining the SQ3R strategy was given and the patient was asked to follow these steps while reading a two-page magazine article. The patient required minimal cues to follow the procedure outline. He was encouraged to highlight main points and important details in the article and cautioned not to over-highlight. The patient answered questions regarding content of the article with 95% accuracy after a 15-minute delay. A handout summarizing the SQ3R strategy was given to the patient for future reference, and he was encouraged to use this strategy when reading his textbook material for class.

SESSION #3

Mnemonic strategies. The patient recalled three mnemonic strategies and adequately demonstrated strategy use given a list of items to recall. The mnemonic strategy use goal was met this session. The patient showed class notes to the clinician to demonstrate how he used these strategies to review class notes and to study for examinations.

Memory book. Upon request, the patient was able to locate information quickly in his memory book. He kept the book well organized and had recorded information in correct sections of his book. The patient reported no scheduling errors since his last session, and the test/project schedule appeared to be up to date. He reported that he felt much more organized in class now that he had a consistent place to record and retrieve information. He also reported that his personal finances were "under control" now that he had a system to record receipt and payment of bills. The patient recorded important information presented during this treatment session in the appropriate sections of his book.

Reading comprehension. The patient answered "wh" content questions regarding the article read during the previous treatment session with 90% accuracy with no review. The patient brought a textbook he was required to read for one of his classes. He adequately followed the SQ3R procedure. The patient spontaneously referred to a handout in his memory book to cue himself regarding procedure. After a 30-minute delay, the patient was able to recall 18 out of 20 details (90%) presented in the chapter. The patient met his reading goal this session.

6

Telephone Interviews with Caregivers Regarding Memory Book System Use after Discharge

The telephone interview procedure described here was used after patients were discharged from individual and/or group therapy to determine if the individuals continued to use their memory book systems in the home environment. The periodic telephone contacts not only proved to be beneficial in collecting data but also provided an opportunity to encourage family/caregivers in reinforcing memory book use.

In the follow-up study conducted by the authors, one patient increased the effective use of the system from week three to week six. The caregiver reported that the patient began using the system more consistently after the first telephone checkup. Therefore, it may be beneficial to include periodic telephone contact with the family, caregiver, and patient to encourage the patient's use of the memory book system.

Procedure

Telephone interviews were conducted with patients' primary caregivers after patients were discharged from therapy to determine if patients continued to use their memory book systems. Interviews with the patients' caregivers were conducted 3 weeks, 6 weeks, 12 weeks, and 24 weeks post discharge. The interviews were conducted according to the script given below.

Interview Script

I am calling to see how _____ (*patient's name*) is doing with his/her memory book system. I am trying to determine how much patients use their books after treatment is completed. Please answer the questions as accurately and honestly as possible.

1. Does (*patient's name*) continue to use his/her memory book system at home/school/work?

    ___ no   ___ yes

2. Do you think he/she uses it as effectively, more effectively, or less effectively now as compared to when he/she was discharged from treatment?

___ as effectively ___ more effectively ___ less effectively

Comments from caregivers: _____

_____

Patient Profile

Ten patients who had successfully learned to use a memory book system independently were chosen for the follow-up interview. (Patients with degenerative diseases were not included in this project because their skills were expected to decline over time.)

Upon discharge, the ten patients, ranging in age from 21 to 72 years, were using their memory book systems independently at home, work, and/or school. The severity of memory impairments varied. All of the patients had time management and information management difficulties secondary to poor memory and organizational skills. Four of the patients had experienced closed head injuries, one patient had had anoxia secondary to cardiac arrest, and five patients were diagnosed with right CVAs.

Results

The results of the telephone interview indicated that 70% of the patients continued to use their memory book systems daily up to 24 weeks post discharge from therapy. As reported by caregivers, 60% of the patients were using their books as effectively as they had been at discharge. The caregivers of the patients who were judged to be less effective memory book users 24 weeks post discharge reported that the patients used the system less often and required more cues to record and retrieve information from the books as compared to their ability to use the system at discharge.

The two patients who were not using their systems daily after 24 weeks were relying on family members to cue them to manage their time, as reported by their caregivers. Both of these patients were unemployed and stayed home during the day with family.

It was surprising that none of the caregivers reported that any of the patients had lost their memory books, which is a common problem when system use training is underway. One patient left the book at school, but it was returned the next day.

Summary of Telephone Interview

Results of Telephone Interview 3 Weeks Post Discharge from Treatment

100% were using the system daily
  0% were not using the system daily

90% were using the system as effectively
  0% were using the system more effectively
10% were using the system less effectively

Results of Telephone Interview 6 Weeks Post Discharge from Treatment

100% were using the system daily
  0% were not using the system daily

80% were using the system as effectively
10% were using the system more effectively
10% were using the system less effectively

Results of Telephone Interview 12 Weeks Post Discharge from Treatment

90% were using the system daily
10% were not using the system daily

70% were using the system as effectively
10% were using the system more effectively
20% were using the system less effectively

Results of Telephone Interview 24 Weeks Post Discharge from Treatment

70% were using the system daily
20% were not using the system daily

60% were using the system as effectively
  0% were using the system more effectively
30% were using the system less effectively

(One patient had had a second stroke and was in the hospital.)

7 Therapy Worksheets

Introduction to the Worksheets

Two types of reproducible worksheets are included in this chapter: mnemonic worksheets that help teach clients various mnemonic strategies, and memory book worksheets, that will help train patients in recording and accessing information in their individual memory book systems.

Mnemonic Worksheets

Mnemonic strategies are most beneficial for recalling lists or sequences of items. The most practical application for using these strategies is in studying lecture or text materials. The worksheets in this chapter are examples of how to use specific mnemonic strategies to aid in recalling information. You should develop individualized worksheets that are applicable to each patient's needs. Use the content of class lecture notes and texts to create additional mnemonic worksheets for each individual.

Memory Book Worksheets

The memory book recording worksheets in this section give structured practice in teaching patients where to record information in their memory books. Encourage patients to refer to their memory books when determining where to record the information. These worksheets can be used in group or individual treatment sessions. In group sessions, encourage patients to think of their own scenarios to present to the group. The group then determines the best section of their books in which to place the information.

Some of the worksheets are divided into levels and progress to more complicated scenarios which may require that the patient record information in several sections of the book. You are encouraged to develop your own worksheets that apply directly to your patients.

You can role-play situations to give patients practice in retrieving and recording information in their books. For example, if a patient has a doctor's appointment scheduled in the near future, you may assist the patient in developing a list of questions to ask the doctor. The patient places the list in the memory book, and you can role-play with the patient, using the book to retrieve the questions and record the answers.

First-Letter Association
Level 1

Make up a word or sentence using the first letters of the key words in each item on the list. The following are examples:

You have to complete the following errands:

- Take the lamp to be repaired.
- Pick up tickets at the travel agency.
- Take the dog to the veterinarian.

The key words may be **l**amp, **t**ickets, and **d**og. The first letters of the key words are **L**, **T**, and **D**. Your mnemonic may be:

"**L**ots **T**o **D**o"

You need to buy lettuce, apples, milk, and bread at the store. The first letters of these words spell lamb. This acronym will help you remember the grocery items once you get to the store.

1. Make up your own word or sentence to remember the following lists:

Grocery list:

- peanuts   • hamburger   • onions   • napkins   • envelopes

Mnemonic: _____

2. First-letter association mnemonics can help you remember errands you need to complete during the day. Think of a mnemonic for the following errands:

- Take laundry to the dry cleaner.
- Buy birthday present.
- Take books to the library.
- Get a battery for the watch.

Key Words:_____

Mnemonic: _____

3. Think of a first-letter association mnemonic to help you remember steps to complete tasks. Write down a mnemonic for the two examples here.

Steps to start microwave:

- Push "cook" button.
- Select temperature level.
- Select cooking time.
- Push "start" button.

Key Words:_____

Mnemonic: _____

Steps to programming a video cassette recorder (VCR):

- Turn on the VCR.
- Put in a blank tape.
- Push " program" button.
- Enter day to record program.
- Enter time to start program recording.
- Enter time to stop program recording.
- Turn off VCR.

Key Words:_____

Mnemonic: _____

4. Write down your "to do" or errand list for today. Then think of a first-letter mnemonic association for your list.

_____

_____

_____

_____

_____

Key Words:_____

Mnemonic: _____

First-Letter Association
Level 2

First-letter association mnemonics can also be used to remember lengthier, more complicated material. You can use this strategy to remember an outline for an oral presentation you are giving, long lists of information, or steps to complete tasks.

Imagine that you are to memorize the arrangement of the motor and sensory functions on the cortex of the brain for a science class you are taking. You need to remember the following list of body parts in order:

- thigh
- arm
- trunk
- shoulder
- hand
- thumb
- neck
- face
- tongue

With the first letter from each word, you may come up with the following mnemonic: "The thin Saudi Arabian had three new fancy Triumphs." This sentence will be easier to remember than the long list of body parts, especially since they need to be remembered in order.

Practice using first-letter association mnemonics for the following examples.

1. The heart is responsible for four functions. They are:

- pumping blood to the lungs
- pumping blood throughout the body
- regulating heart rate
- regulating blood pressure

Key Words:_____

Mnemonic: _____

2. Life cycle of the butterfly

- egg
- caterpillar
- pupa
- adult

Mnemonic: _____

3. The process of cell division occurs in six basic steps. These steps are:

- Chromosomes appear as long threads.
- The chromosomes pair up and form bivalents.
- The chromosome copies itself. These copies are called chromatids.
- The chromatids swap sections. This process is called crossing over.
- The pairs of chromatids in each bivalent split apart. The cell divides once.
- The cell divides again. Each of the four new cells has half the chromosomes that the original cell had.

Key words: _____

Mnemonic: _____

_____

_____

4. Nerves of the skin

- pressure-sensitive endings
- cold receptors
- heat receptors
- touch receptors
- nerve endings sensitive to pain

Key words: _____

Mnemonic: _____

_____

5. Standard scale of hardness

- talc
- gypsum
- calcite
- fluorite
- apatite
- feldspar
- quartz
- topaz
- corundum
- diamond

Mnemonic: _____

_____

6. Look at your current lecture notes and the chapters in the textbooks you are currently reading. Write lists of items you need to remember from your notes or textbook material. Make up first-letter association mnemonics for each list.

_____

_____

_____

_____

Storytelling
Level 1

Storytelling involves making up a story to associate items you need to remember. This mnemonic system works because most people find it easier to recall a story than a series of unrelated words.

Imagine you have to go to the store and buy apples, soup, and rubber bands. A story using these might be: "I found a rubber band in my apple soup." Drawing a picture of this image would help you remember these items.

Some people find it easier to write grocery items and errands on a list when they go shopping, whereas others prefer using mnemonic strategies.

Practice using the storytelling strategy by making up a story for the following lists.

1. You need to take the following items to your friend on Sunday:

   • dessert   • chicken soup   • candles

Story:_____

_____

_____

_____

2. You need to buy the following items at the hardware store:

   • hammer   • electrical tape   • screws   • red spray paint

Story:_____

_____

_____

_____

3. You need to buy the following items for tonight's dinner:

- tomatoes
- onions
- green peppers
- shrimp
- whipped cream

Story:_____

_____

_____

_____

4. You're speaking at the city council meeting tomorrow night. You want to make sure you cover the following points in your presentation:

- dog leash law
- parking fines
- building permits
- zoning
- trash collection

Story:_____

_____

_____

_____

5. You need to buy the following items at the drug store:

- toothpaste
- shampoo
- razors
- aspirin

Story:_____

_____

_____

_____

Storytelling
Level 2

Practice the storytelling memory strategy by making up a story using the following examples. Remember, it is easier to recall a story than a series of unrelated words.

1. You need to remember the following information about Norway for a test you are taking tomorrow:

   - It is a kingdom in northern Europe.
   - It is 125,000 square miles in area.
   - It is on the Scandinavian Peninsula.
   - The capital is Oslo.

   Key Words:_____

   _____

   _____

   Story:_____

   _____

   _____

   _____

2. Next week, you will speak about birds to a group of 4-H members. You are studying the parts of birds just in case someone asks you a question about it.

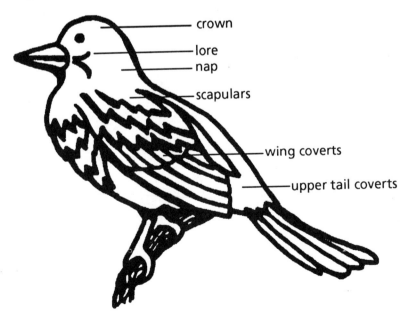

crown

lore

nap

scapulars

wing coverts

upper tail coverts

Story:_____

_____

_____

_____

3. You are giving a presentation to a grade-school music club. They have asked you to make a presentation about the Beatles, a rock band. You need to know the following facts for your presentation:

- John Lennon was born in 1940.
- Paul McCartney was born in 1942.
- Ringo Starr was born in 1940.
- George Harrison was born in 1943.
- Ringo Starr's original name was Richard Starkey.

Story:_____

_____

_____

_____

4. You have to remember the following bones of the skull for the science test scheduled for tomorrow. They are:

- temporal bone
- parietal bone
- frontal bone
- sphenoid bone

Story:_____

_____

_____

_____

5. You have a health test scheduled for tomorrow afternoon. Part of a classroom lecture was on the parts of the eye. You need to remember the following eye parts:

- iris
- pupil
- cornea
- lens

Story:_____

_____

_____

_____

Loci Mnemonics

Loci mnemonics involves visualizing a series of locations in a logical order, then visualizing items to be remembered at each specific location. Drawing the locations on paper can help you remember them. Use the same set of locations for each list of items you need to remember.

1. Determine a set of four locations. Choose familiar locations such as places in your house or apartment. Draw a picture of the locations below:

_____   _____

_____   _____

2. Now try to visualize the following items at each location.

   • milk   • butter   • lettuce   • cheese

Wait 15 minutes and look back at your location drawings. See if you can remember the four grocery items. You may want to draw the grocery items at each location on a separate piece of paper as you practice.

3. Use this strategy for the following errand list. Visualize an item related to each errand at your locations.

   • Pick up dry cleaning.   • Call telephone repair person.
   • Get a picture framed.   • Buy a shower curtain.

4. Look at the items on your grocery list or "to do" list. Now visualize each item at your above locations. You may need to add locations if you have more than four items.

   _____

   _____

   _____

Remembering Names and Faces

Make an association between the following peoples' names and their appearance. Then create a mental picture of the association. If the name has no meaning, substitute words that sound similar. Draw (or have someone else draw) the association in the boxes below to help remember the association. An example is shown:

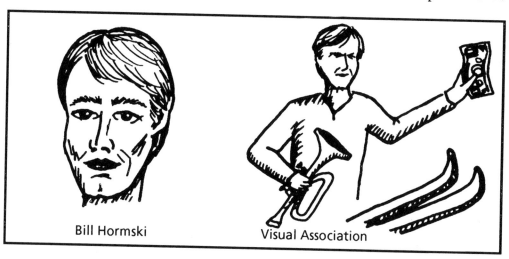

Bill Hormski   Visual Association

Practice using this strategy for someone you have met recently (therapists, doctors, friends). Use a photograph, if available, to make an association and mental image.

Name: _____ Relationship: _____

Association: _____

(continued)

The following suggestions will help in recall of peoples' names:

- When someone is introducing a person, listen carefully to the person's name. Ask for the name to be repeated if you did not hear it.
- After you hear the name, repeat it several times to yourself.
- Spell the name out loud or to yourself.
- Associate the person's name with something about the way that person looks or acts. Substitute words for names that have no meaning.
- Occasionally rehearse the visual image or substitute words. Drawing your visual image on paper may make the association stronger.

Organization
Level 1

Organized information is easier to learn than unorganized information. If you are memorizing lists, try to categorize or group them in some way that makes sense to you. Practice this strategy by completing the following assignment.

Directions

Read all the words in each group.
Determine how the items are similar or different.
Write the name of each category.
Separate the words into categories.
Rehearse the names of the categories and the items in each category.

1. These items belong to which two categories?

_____ _____

- table   - eraser   - pencil
- chair   - marker   - couch

List the items under the appropriate categories:

Category:_____ Category: _____

- _____   - _____

- _____   - _____

- _____   - _____

Rehearse the category names and the items in each category at least three times. Turn over the page and write down all six of the items.

(continued)

2. These items belong to which two categories?

_____   _____

- jeans   • hoe   • rake
- shorts   • spade   • T-shirt

List the items under the appropriate categories:

Category:_____   Category: _____

- _____   • _____

- _____   • _____

- _____   • _____

Rehearse the category names and the items in each category at least three times. Turn over the page and write down all six of the items.

3. These items belong to which two categories?

_____   _____

- toilet paper   • oranges   • apples
- paper towels   • napkins   • lemons

List the items under the appropriate categories:

Category:_____   Category: _____

- _____   • _____

- _____   • _____

- _____   • _____

Rehearse the category names and the items in each category at least three times. Turn over the page and write down all six of the items.

Organization
Level 2

Directions

Read all the words in each group. Determine how the items are similar or different. Write the name of each category. Separate the words into categories. Rehearse the names of the categories and the items in each category.

1. The items listed below belong to which three categories?

_____   _____   _____

• baseball	• pink	• soda pop
• coffee	• purple	• soccer
• basketball	• milk	• football
• white	• orange juice	• green

List the items under the appropriate categories:

Category:_____   Category:_____   Category:_____

•_____   •_____   •_____

•_____   •_____   •_____

•_____   •_____   •_____

•_____   •_____   •_____

Rehearse the category names and the items in each category at least three times. Turn over the page and write down all twelve of the items.

(continued)

2. The items listed below belong to which three categories?

_____   _____   _____

- noodles
- eggs
- plastic knives
- cheese

- flour
- hamburger
- butter
- plastic spoons

- paper plates
- salt
- tomato sauce
- napkins

List the items under the appropriate categories:

Category:_____   Category:_____   Category:_____

- _____   - _____   - _____

- _____   - _____   - _____

- _____   - _____   - _____

- _____   - _____   - _____

Rehearse the category names and the items in each category at least three times. Turn over the page and write down all twelve of the items.

On a separate sheet of paper, make a list of items you need to remember. Use a grocery list,"to do" list, or items from your classroom notes. Organize the items into categories.

SQ3R Reading Strategy

SQ3R is a mnemonic for: Survey, Question, Read, Recall, and Review. Choose an article of interest or a portion of a textbook chapter that has recently been assigned to you. Use the worksheet below to assist you in using this strategy.

Survey

Skim over the reading material. Pay attention to bold words, headings, and pictures. What do you think this reading material is about?

_____

_____

_____

Question

Skim the reading material a second time. Think of five important questions about the text (*who, what, when, where, why*, or *how*). Write your questions below.

_____

_____

_____

_____

_____

Read

Read the written material in its entirety. Look for the answers to your questions as you read.

Recall

Recite the main points and details presented in the reading material. Write the answers to your questions below.

1. _____

_____

2. _____

_____

3. _____

_____

(continued)

4. _____

_____

5. _____

_____

6. _____

Write down key words and phrases as you summarize the material.

_____

_____

_____

_____

_____

Review

Review what you have read. Look back to the text if you cannot remember something. Look at your questions and notes above. State the main points and details aloud.

Recording Information
Level 1

Memory Book Sections

Daily schedule: something that happens at a specific time

To do: something that needs to be done sometime during the day

Reference: information you will need to keep for a long time

Notes: information that is being given to you verbally

Directions

Indicate in which section of your book you would record the following information.

1. Your social security number.

   _____

2. You need to buy craft glue.

   _____

3. You need to pick up your medicine at the drug store.

   _____

4. You need to call your friend and remind her to bring a dessert to your party tomorrow.

   _____

5. You are picking your friend up at the airport on Saturday at 10:25 p.m.

   _____

6. You have a dentist appointment on Thursday at 3:00 p.m.

   _____

7. You need to call the repair person to fix your dishwasher.

   _____

8. You need to go to the post office to pick up a package.

   _____

9. Your friend just moved, and her new phone number is 555-5474.

   _____

(continued)

10. Your insurance agent is Ed Martin.

_____

11. Your physician gave you a new medicine, and you need to take it at 8:00 a.m. and 8:00 p.m.

_____

12. Your physician told you that the medicine he gave you should help decrease the pain you are having in your leg.

_____

13. Your friend is telling you how to get to her new apartment. She says, "Go north on 342nd and take a left at Pine Street. Go about four blocks, and my house is the big white house on the corner of 346th and Pine."

_____

14. You are invited to a baby shower next Friday at 4:00 p.m.

_____

15. You need to call Joe tomorrow at work.

_____

16. You have been assigned locker number 12 at the gym. The combination of your lock is 12-30-12.

_____

17. You need to register to vote.

_____

18. Your dog has an appointment at the veterinarian's office at 9:00 a.m. this Wednesday.

_____

19. You were impressed with your friend's new electric typewriter, and you want to buy one just like it. You want to remember the name and model number of the typewriter.

_____

20. You just finished your physical therapy session, and your therapist is reviewing a new exercise you are to practice two times a day. You want to make sure you remember how to do the exercise and how often you are to practice it.

_____

Recording Information
Level 2

Directions

Indicate in which section of your memory book (schedule, to do today, reference, or notes) you would record the following information:

1. You need to call your travel agent to cancel your flight that is scheduled to leave on Friday afternoon at 4:30 p.m.

   _____

2. You are purchasing a new computer, and the salesperson is showing you how to hook up the new system.

   _____

3. You are picking a friend up at her house tomorrow at 6:00 p.m. It takes $1\frac{1}{2}$ hours to get to her house. She wants you to telephone her before you leave.

   _____

4. Your aunt from California called to tell you that she moved and that her new phone number is (304) 555-3950.

   _____

5. The pool hours at the recreation center have changed. The old hours were 8:00 a.m. to 6:00 p.m. The pool will now be open from 9:00 a.m. to 4:00 p.m. Monday through Friday, and 11:00 a.m. to 3:00 p.m. on Saturday and Sunday.

   _____

6. Your art class has been canceled today.

   _____

7. You are making dinner for a friend tonight. The recipe you are using tells you to marinate the chicken for 3 hours and 15 minutes.

   _____

(continued)

8. You received a notice in the mail today stating that your electric bill is past due. You are sure that you paid it.

   _____

9. You go to pay your bills and realize you are on your last book of checks.

   _____

10. You received an invitation to a friend's wedding in the mail today. Your friend is getting married on a day that you are scheduled to work. You want to ask your boss during your lunch break tomorrow if you can have the day off.

    _____

11. You just purchased a new home vacuum system. The sales representative demonstrates how to replace the bags and tells you where to take your system if you need to have it repaired or serviced.

    _____

12. You are leaving on vacation next Wednesday at 3:00 p.m. You need to pick up your plane ticket from Lifestyles Travel on Monday between 9:00 a.m. and 4:00 p.m.

    _____

13. You are looking for an apartment to rent. A friend of yours tells you that there is a new service in town that will provide you with a computer printout of all the apartments in the area in your price range. The service is free.

    _____

14. The remote control for your television is not working. You purchased the set over a year ago, and you are not sure if your warranty is still good. You have the warranty in a file at work.

    _____

15. The salesperson at the shoe store tells you to add 1 tablespoon of vinegar to the shoe dye solution you are purchasing. She explains that the vinegar makes the dye spread more evenly when applied.

    _____

16. For your birthday, your aunt sent you a $20.00 gift certificate to a local restaurant, your friend gave you a set of towels, and your neighbor baked you a pie.

_____

17. You are watching television, and you see an advertisement for a juice machine. You have been thinking about buying a juicer, and the one on television sounds as if it is a good deal. The announcer tells you to call the number on the screen for more information.

_____

18. You just had the oil changed in your car. You will need to take your car back to the station when your odometer reaches 18,000 miles.

_____

19. You are making dinner for some friends next Saturday night. You need to plan the menu and make a shopping list.

_____

20. You are watching a cooking show on television, and you want to remember how to make the chocolate cake that is being demonstrated.

_____

Recording Information
Level 3

Directions

Indicate in which section of your memory book (schedule, to do today, reference, or notes) you would record the following information.

1. The copy machine at work is broken. Your boss tells you to telephone the photocopy repair shop first thing in the morning. You need to give the repair shop the make, model number, and warranty number when you telephone.

   _____

2. You purchased several plants at a local nursery. The salesperson told you how often to water each plant, the type of fertilizer to use, and the amount of sunlight each plant requires. He also suggested that they be transplanted into larger pots and told you the type of soil you need to purchase.

   _____

3. You attended a class on how to invest your savings. The instructor presented three investment options that you were interested in pursuing. After class, you asked the instructor for more information about these investment options. The instructor suggested that you contact a financial consultant and gave you the names of three reputable consultants in your area.

   _____

4. You are meeting a friend tomorrow for a game of golf at 8:00 a.m. You realize that you have a dentist appointment scheduled at 10:00 a.m. for the same day. You want to reschedule the golf game for Saturday.

   _____

5. You purchased tickets to the symphony for tomorrow night's performance. You just discovered you lost the tickets.

   _____

6. Your new electric typewriter has memory storage, and you can program your patients' addresses in the computer's memory. Every time you use the typewriter, you forget the sequence of keys you need to press to store and retrieve the addresses. The sequence for storing addresses is "ADD" + "CODE" + "STORE." The sequence for retrieving addresses is "CODE" + "STORE" + "GET."

   _____

7. Your friend is getting married, and you volunteered to help him plan the wedding. He asked you to obtain tuxedo measurements from all of the ushers. He gave you the names of the ushers and their phone numbers.

_____

8. You are purchasing a new car, and you need to obtain financing. The car dealer is offering an 8.5% interest rate. You need to call banks to determine if you can obtain a better rate.

_____

9. You are on the phone with a loan officer, and he tells you that in order to qualify for a loan from your bank, you need to provide him with a copy of last year's tax return, a current paycheck stub, last month's banking statement, and current credit card statements.

_____

10. You are going shopping with a friend today. You are meeting her at a new discount store at 1:00 p.m. It will take you about 45 minutes to get to the store from your house.

_____

11. You are picking up a friend at the airport on Friday at 6:30 p.m. You are not sure how to get to the airport, so you telephone your brother and he gives you directions.

_____

12. You have an appointment to get your suit altered at 5:00 p.m. tomorrow. You receive a phone call from the alteration shop, and you are informed that they need to change your appointment because the seamstress is ill.

_____

13. You have not spoken to your cousin in three years. She telephones you to see how you are doing.

_____

14. Your doctor wants you to monitor the pain you are having in your leg. He has asked you to keep a chart and to rate the pain on a scale of 1 to 10. You are to rate the pain in the morning and at night.

_____

(continued)

15. You have an opportunity to get tickets to a concert you want to attend. Tickets are limited, and you have to go to the ticket office between 3:00 p.m. and 5:00 p.m. next Thursday to purchase tickets. You have to work next Thursday afternoon. You want to call your friend to see if he could get the tickets for you.

   _____

16. Your electric furnace stopped working last night, and you called a repair person to come and fix it. Your friend is a retired electrician, and he tells you a list of questions to ask the repair person upon arrival.

   _____

17. Your doctor changed your medication from 200 mg two times a day to 100 mg three times a day. You are to take your new prescription at breakfast, lunch, and dinner. You were instructed to call your doctor immediately if you experience dizziness.

   _____

18. Your cable company called to inform you that you will be billed for cable every two months instead of every month.

   _____

19. Your watch broke, so you took it to a repair shop. The repair person informed you that he was unable to repair it. He suggested that you send the watch back to the manufacturer. He gave you the address and phone number of the watch manufacturer.

   _____

20. You have agreed to house sit for a friend who is leaving town on Saturday and is returning in two weeks. He calls you at work and asks you to water his plants, feed his cat twice a day (dry food in the morning, canned food at night), get his mail from the post office, and take the garbage out Tuesday night. He is going to bring his house key to you tomorrow at 4:00 pm.

   _____

Retrieving Information

The following exercise is designed to give the patient the opportunity to practice accessing information in the memory book system upon demand and to increase efficiency of memory book use.

Ask the patient the following questions. Record the patient's responses using the following response codes:

SR = spontaneous response   SC = specific cue needed

NC = no cue needed   GC = gestural cue needed

NSC = nonspecific cue needed   M = model needed

1. When is your next occupational therapy appointment?

   _____

2. What do you have scheduled for tomorrow at 3:00 p.m.?

   _____

3. What are the names of your therapists?

   _____

4. When was your last scheduled appointment?

   _____

5. What activity did you work on in your last speech therapy appointment?

   _____

6. How many times did you attend physical therapy last week?

   _____

7. What are your occupational therapy goals?

   _____

8. How many items have you completed on your "to do" list for today?

   _____

(continued)

9. What do you do if you are unable to complete all of the items on the "to do" list in one day?

_____

10. What is your doctor's name?

_____

11. What medications do you take and why?

_____

12. When do you take your medications?

_____

13. What appointments do you have tomorrow afternoon?

_____

14. What is your home address and phone number?

_____

15. When was your injury or illness?

_____

16. What is today's date?

_____

17. What was your last homework/therapy assignment?

_____

18. What day of the week was the day before yesterday?

_____

School-Related Scenarios

Directions

Locate the page in your memory book where you would make a note if the following situation occurred. Tell what you would write on that page.

1. Your teacher gave you a math assignment, and it is due tomorrow.

2. Your library book is due next Friday.

3. Science class will be held in room 22 next week.

4. There is a new grading policy for class.

5. Your teacher is giving a lecture on the Western Movement.

6. You need a permission slip from your parent for a class trip.

7. Your book report due date has been extended by one week.

8. You have a new teacher for science class.

9. You have two new projects due next week.

10. Your locker number has been changed.

11. You need to bring felt pens and a ruler from home for a class project.

12. Your teacher informs your class that all students must bring paper and pencils to class each day.

13. You are meeting a friend at 6:00 p.m. at the basketball game Friday.

14. Your score was 85% on today's math quiz.

15. You will not be riding the bus home from school as planned. You are to wait for your ride in front of the school after your last class.

16. You do not understand an assignment that was given to you by your teacher. You need to ask your teacher about the assignment before you go home from school.

17. Your friend asked you to call him tonight at 7:30.

18. You were invited to a concert this weekend. You want to remind yourself to ask permission to go.

19. School elections are tomorrow during second period.

20. You need to bring $3.00 for the field trip next week.

19. What is the name of the last school you attended?

_____

20. When is your next therapy appointment?

_____

Total score: Indicate the number of times each response was given out of 20 items.

_____ *Spontaneous response:* Patient spontaneously answered question without looking in memory book.

_____ *No cues:* Patient located information in memory book without cues.

_____ *Nonspecific cues:* Patient required nonspecific cues to locate answers in the memory book.

_____ *Specific cues:* Patient required specific cues to locate answers in the memory book.

_____ *Gestural cues:* Patient required a gestural cue (clinician pointed to correct section of book).

_____ *Model:* Clinician located information in the client's book and pointed to it.

Handouts...
- *Family Members* • *Caregivers*
- *Employers* • *Staff Trainers* • *Teachers*
- *School Staff Members* • *Students/Clients*

- **Handouts for Family Members and Caregivers**
  - The Brain and Memory
  - Severe Memory Loss and Confusion
  - Memory Book System Use at Home
  - General Suggestions for Communicating with
    Individuals Who Have Memory Impairments
  - Using Visual Cues in the Home
  - Improving Pathfinding Skills

- **Handout for Employers and Staff Trainers**
  - Using Memory Strategies on the Job

- **Handouts for Teachers and School Staff Members**
  - Memory Book System Use at School
  - Brain Injury and Cognitive Impairments
  - Memory Strategies in the Classroom

- **Handouts for Students/Clients**
  - Classroom Note Taking
  - Understanding What You Have Read
  - General Memory Techniques
  - Study Reminders Checklist

The Brain and Memory

No one structure or location in the brain is responsible for memory. Rather, memory is a complex process. The brain uses different processes to store memories of what you see, hear, feel, smell, and taste.

There appear to be three phases involved in memory. The first phase is sensory memory. In this stage, your senses hold on to information very briefly. This sensory information is then processed by the brain and stored into short-term memory. Short-term memory consists of what you have in mind at the moment.

The amount of information that can be stored in short-term memory is limited. The information can be kept in this storage for only a short period of time (30 seconds or less). Because the amount of information that can be held in short-term memory is limited, much of the information in this storage system is lost, discarded, or ignored. If you are not able to hold on to information for a few seconds, you probably will not be able to remember the information several hours or days later.

Information in short-term memory is then processed and transferred to long-term storage. Long-term memory has the capacity to hold a large amount of information. Information can be stored in long-term memory from 30 seconds to a lifetime. Memories from yesterday and from childhood are stored in long-term memory.

Some degree of memory impairment is present in many people who have experienced brain damage. Damage to the brain can occur from a stroke, head trauma, brain infection, or disease.

Memory affects almost every daily activity. Many times, people with memory difficulties will have problems attending and concentrating. They become easily distracted by noises (such as people talking, children crying, television or radio audio, and so forth). They may also find it difficult to concentrate when visual distractions are present (such as people walking by, children playing, or cars going by the window). It is important to decrease or eliminate these distractions when the person is trying to concentrate on a task.

Severe Memory Loss and Confusion

Develop a consistent daily routine for bathing, dressing, meals, and so forth. Give the individual as much freedom as possible to allow the person to have a sense of independence, but provide enough structure to help decrease confusion. A written daily schedule will help provide structure.

Avoid talking about the individual's problems or impairments in front of the person, and gently remind others to do the same.

Try to maintain a relaxed, calm atmosphere. If the individual becomes upset, speak in a soft, calm voice. Sometimes playing soft music will help the person relax. Check to make sure the individual always wears an identification bracelet or necklace with the phone number and the nature of the problem.

Avoid too much stimulation. Keep the individual active and provide stimulating activities, but realize that too much activity or stimulation can be upsetting.

The person may laugh, cry, or have inappropriate verbal outbursts. The individual may try to strike out physically at people who are assisting with an activity, or refuse to complete daily activities. These reactions are caused by the brain damage. Watch for signs that the individual is becoming upset or overwhelmed.

The person may overreact to situations or events, especially if a task is too complicated or if the individual is asked to do more than one thing at a time. Simplify activities, breaking them down into simple steps.

Look for activities the individual enjoys and is able to participate in, and make use of those activities.

Be a good observer. Look for signs that may indicate that the individual is becoming upset, and try to determine the trigger for the behavior. Try to avoid the activity or event that triggered the behavior and, if possible, simplify or change the activity.

If the individual becomes upset or resistant, gently try to remove the person from the environment. Remain calm and move slowly. Do not reason or argue with the individual. Remember, the inappropriate behavior is due to the brain damage, and the person is not behaving this way intentionally.

Take time out from being a caregiver. Schedule some time for yourself on a regular basis.

Memory Book System Use at Home

A memory book system is designed to help individuals with memory impairments compensate for their memory problems so they can be as independent as possible. There are different types and sizes of memory books. The book is individualized for each person depending on that person's needs. It is important for the clinician(s) to know the person's household responsibilities and lifestyle, employment, and activity demands when establishing a memory book system. Family members and caregivers may be asked to assist in the development of the memory book system.

Most memory books consist of several sections. The individual is taught to accurately and consistently record important information in the book that the person will need to remember in the future (such as the medication schedule, therapy appointments, upcoming birthdays, daily routine, things to do). The book is organized so that it is easy to find the information when needed. The clinician(s) will work on activities that teach the individual how the book is organized, and how to record and retrieve information in the book.

It is important that family members and caregivers assist in memory book training. For the patient to learn to use a memory book system successfully, family and caregivers must be supportive of its use. Training must be broken down into small steps that can be easily learned. Everyone involved in training must respond consistently.

Keep in mind that individuals with memory impairments may take longer to learn new tasks. Training steps may need to be repeated over and over before they are learned. Be patient, and don't give up. Most importantly, be consistent and follow the written treatment plan provided by the clinician(s). Try to provide as many opportunities to use the memory book system as you can. If you have questions or suggestions, write them down and share them with the clinician(s).

General Suggestions for Communicating with Individuals Who Have Memory Impairments

- If possible, decrease distractions in the home, school, or work environment when having a conversation or giving instructions, or when the individual is completing a task requiring concentration.

- Get the individual's attention and face the individual before initiating conversation or giving verbal instructions.

- Avoid giving lengthy verbal instructions or using complex sentences and vocabulary. Break instructions down into simple step-by-step tasks. Written steps may be helpful for the individual when completing a task.

- The individual may not remember information discussed in conversation, even immediately after the information has been given. The person may need to have the information repeated several times in several different ways. Avoid making judgmental comments if the individual forgets something you just said.

- The individual's ability to remember and concentrate may fluctuate over time. You may see the person's skills deteriorate if the individual is tired.

- Use descriptions to help the individual orient to person, place, and time.

- If the individual has difficulty remembering names, state your name instead of asking the person to recall your name.

Using Visual Cues in the Home

Using cues in the home can assist individuals with memory impairments to become more independent. The use of cues in the home should be based on the individual's needs as observed by family members and rehabilitation professionals.

Suggested Visual Cues

- Label the doors inside the house. Individuals with memory impairment may have difficulty remembering where the bathroom, bedroom, den, or sewing room is located in the home. Hallways with several doors tend to be especially confusing. Pairing a picture cue with the word cue makes it easier for the individual to locate the desired room.

- Put labels on drawers, cupboards, and cabinets to label their contents. If the individual has difficulty understanding written words alone, pair a picture cue with the written word. Try not to change the contents of drawers or cupboards. It is important to keep items in the same place to help develop an association between the object and where it is to be kept. It may be beneficial to place labels on the tops of dressers or tables to indicate where certain items should be returned. For example, if an individual usually keeps keys on the coffee table in the living room, place a label on the table to help remind the person to put the keys back in the same location after use.

- Use markers on thermostats, air conditioners, hearing aids, heating pads, electric blankets, TV channel changers, oven dials, and so forth to indicate appropriate settings. Large, brightly colored markers that are easily seen tend to work best. Consult with a professional if you are unsure whether it is safe for the individual to use certain electrical appliances.

- Write out simple instructions for using appliances and equipment or for completing activities. Keep the instructions simple, and write them out step by step. Place the written instructions next to the appliance/equipment. Some individuals find it easier to use a checklist system in which they are required to check off each step as they complete it. This helps them attend to which step they are on.

- Use night lights in the house. Some individuals with memory impairments experience more difficulty when first waking up and may be more disoriented at night. Reflector tape placed at intervals from the bedroom to the bathroom may also assist them in finding their way to the bathroom at night.

- Place clocks at easy viewing locations throughout the house. This will help assist the individual in orienting to time. If the person has difficulty reading a clock face, use digital clocks. Large digital and face clocks that are easy to read are available (ask your clinician for suggestions on where to purchase these clocks in your area).

- Use calendars to help the individual orient to the current date. Mark off the days on the calendar, and place a movable marker on the current day. (Placing a brightly colored arrow next to the current day works well.) This may help the individual in locating the correct date and decrease frustration.

- Use written schedules to help the individual remember scheduled appointments, daily activities, medication schedules, and so forth. If the patient is in a wheelchair, tape the schedule on the lap tray. Memory book systems and electronic computers are helpful for individuals functioning at higher levels. The clinicians can assist in establishing an organized memory book system based on the individual's needs and skill level.

- Safety checklists located at the front door may help the individual to do a "safety check" to make sure appliances are turned off, heat/air conditioner is turned down, lights are turned off, and so on, before leaving the house. The individual may need training to use the checklist consistently when leaving the home.

- For individuals who have difficulty remembering the names of important people (such as relatives and clinicians), develop a picture book containing biographical information about each person. Periodically review the pictures, cuing the individual to recall the information. Write down an association for the person's name and face, and rehearse the association to enhance recall.

Improving Pathfinding Skills

Here are some suggestions to help individuals compensate for difficulties they may have when attempting to find their way from one location to another.

- Locate maps of buildings, school campuses, cities, and other locales to assist in pathfinding. If none are available, construct your own maps using simple drawings. Put permanent landmarks on the map. Highlight common routes with different colors. Practice using the map to get to different locations.

- Place the maps in plastic sheet covers. The individual can use a dry-erase pen to mark the route on the map, then trace steps back to the original location. This system works well for locating rooms in a building.

- Write simple step-by-step instructions for getting from one location to another. Use permanent landmarks in the instructions. Practice following the written instructions when traveling these routes.

- Mark doors and hallways clearly in buildings. In schools, classroom numbers and teachers' names should be easy to read. Make hallways look different in some way. (For example, hang pictures or posters, or paint different colors.) Keep landmarks consistent in buildings. Avoid changing the location of furniture, pictures on walls, and other identifiable markers.

- Use reflector tape on hallway walls to help the individual locate a frequently traveled route in the building (such as to the bathroom or dining room). Remind the individual to follow the tape line.

- Practice an appropriate procedure to follow if the individual becomes lost. A written cue card placed in the memory book or wallet can be a helpful reminder of the sequence of actions to take if the person becomes lost.

Other: _____

_____

_____

Using Memory Strategies on the Job

Almost everyone uses memory and organizational strategies on the job. These strategies can be especially helpful for individuals with brain injury. Involving the individual in the development of the strategy can make it more meaningful. It may also help the person realize the value of the system. The following are strategies that can be used to help the employee with memory impairments be successful on the job.

- Put visual cues in the environment to help remind the employee to complete tasks. Lists, written instructions, and signs placed at the employee's work station may be helpful.

- Lengthy, complicated tasks should be broken down into a series of small, sequenced steps. A checklist system may be developed and the employee trained in its use.

- When giving the employee a new task, show how to do the task as you explain it. Simple written directions on how to complete the task may be beneficial so the employee can refer to them at a later time.

- Ask the employee to retell directions just given or to demonstrate the task. This way, you are certain the employee understood you, and it also gives the person a chance to rehearse the information.

- Decrease distractions in the work environment if possible. Excessive noise or interruptions can make it more difficult for the employee to concentrate on the job.

- The employee may carry a notebook (sometimes called a memory book) that contains information that is important to remember. It generally consists of a daily schedule, a list of things to do, important telephone numbers, names, and so forth. This book is used to record information that needs to be remembered. The employee may require cues to use the system to record or retrieve information in the book.

(continued)

- The employee may have an electronic wrist watch or alarm system that serves to remind the person to complete tasks or to look at the memory book. Alarms can be useful reminders on the job.

- It is sometimes helpful if a consistent routine can be maintained at work, especially if the employee is learning a new job.

- The employee may ask a question or express a concern over and over several times during the day. The employee may not remember the response that was given previously. It may be helpful to ask the person to write down questions or concerns. Give the employee a response in writing. Ask the employee to put the response in the memory book and to refer to the response if needed.

- Encourage the employee to write down questions or concerns that may come to mind during the work day. During the course of the day, the employee may forget questions or direct them to inappropriate people. If the employee writes them down, the concerns can be reviewed at an appropriate time and with the appropriate person.

- The employee needs to work closely with the job trainer(s) to develop and practice strategies to improve job performance. Role-playing job situations that are problematic, and practicing appropriate verbal responses in a simulated work environment, may be part of the employee's work training program. It is important that you provide consistent and honest feedback to the employee and the employee's job trainer.

Memory Book System Use at School

Student's name: _____

The above student is using a memory book system to help compensate for memory and/or organizational deficits. It is important that all staff members support the use of this system. The book is individualized for the student's needs. Please make suggestions to the therapist(s) regarding ideas you may have to make the book more functional in the classroom. The following are suggestions that will help the student become more independent in using the system.

- Familiarize yourself with the sections and forms in the student's memory book.

- Cue the student to record and retrieve information in the memory book following the cuing hierarchy (nonspecific cue to specific cue).

- For the student to learn to use the memory book independently, teachers and staff must be supportive of its use.

- Follow the written treatment plan provided by the student's clinician(s). You may be asked to keep data on the student's ability to use the memory book in your classroom.

- Provide the student with as many opportunities to use the memory book system as possible. Encourage the student to use the book outside the class environment (library, classroom outings, and so forth).

- The student's parents are encouraged to participate in the memory book training process. Please reinforce the importance of parental involvement in training.

The following sections have been established in this student's book. (Clinician: List the sections that are included in this student's memory book, and provide examples of the type of information to be recorded in each section.)

(continued)

1. _____

_____

2. _____

_____

3. _____

_____

4. _____

_____

5. _____

_____

Clinician(s)' comments: _____

_____

_____

_____

_____

Brain Injury and Cognitive Impairments

Student's name: _____

The above student is currently experiencing learning difficulties as a result of a brain injury. The following is a checklist of difficulties currently being experienced, and suggestions for dealing with these difficulties:

_____ Difficulty concentrating or attending to tasks. The student is easily distractible and has difficulty completing tasks, especially in a noisy environment. Try to decrease distractions as much as possible. Cue the student to listen when important information is being presented in class.

_____ Difficulty initiating activities. The student requires assistance getting started with activities, and frequent prompting to continue with a project or to go on to the next step may be required. The student requires extra cuing; written and verbal cues are beneficial for this student.

_____ Impulsive and acts without thinking. The student may require verbal or written cues to slow down and to think before acting.

_____ Difficulty processing information at a normal rate. The student requires more time to process verbal and written information. The student may not be able to get class assignments done on time because of slow processing.

_____ Easily overwhelmed and has difficulty coping with stress. The student may become agitated by activities that are too complex or stressful. Look for activities or situations that trigger outbursts and make changes in the environment or help the student develop strategies to cope with stress.

_____ Difficulty coping with changes in the environment. The student may easily become upset by changes in a routine or activity. Help the student anticipate change, if possible. Work with the student on being more flexible, accepting of changes, and solving problems as they occur.

(continued)

___ Difficulty organizing and expressing thoughts. The student requires increased time to communicate ideas. The student also requires written cues for organizing writing.

___ Poor time management. The student has difficulty organizing unstructured time. The student may require strategies to help remember to do assignments, bring materials to class, and plan activities that need to be completed in the future. A memory book system has been established to help the student manage time. Cue the student to use this book.

___ Difficulty remembering information and generalizing what has been learned to new situations. The student requires increased practice using what has been learned in a variety of situations.

___ Denies deficits. The student does not believe that skills have changed. The student may have difficulty accepting compensatory strategies, and may not be willing to participate in special programs. Try to involve the student in developing strategies that make learning and remembering easier.

___ Difficulty remembering how to get from one class to another. Remind the student to use the map/written directions to assist with pathfinding.

___ Other: _____

_____

_____

_____

The student's strengths include: _____

_____

_____

_____

_____

_____

_____

Memory Strategies in the Classroom

Student's name: _____

The above student is currently having difficulty remembering information presented in the classroom. The following is a list of suggestions for helping the student compensate for these memory deficits.

- Cue the student to use the memory notebook in class according to the written plan. Reinforce the importance of the system and its use. Encourage the student to write in the memory book important information that needs to be remembered.

- Provide written instructions, checklists, classroom lecture outlines, and other written cues for the student to increase attention and recall.

- Provide the student with extra cues to attend to important information that is being presented.

- Encourage the student to use mnemonic memory strategies in the classroom to aid in recall. The following is a list of several mnemonic strategies that appear to be useful for this student and can easily be incorporated into classroom instruction:

____ *Categorization:* Categorize information or group information in a logical way.

____ *First-letter association:* Develop a word or sentence that is made out of the first letters of the items to be remembered.

____ *Association:* Take information the student already knows and relate it to information the student needs to remember. Comparing and contrasting, rewording information, and relating the information to an experience are examples of association.

____ *Storytelling:* A story is used to associate items to be remembered in a continuous, related sequence.

(continued)

___ *Visualization:* Visualize or picture the items to be remembered on a list.

___ Any combination of the above strategies

___ Other:_____

_____

_____

_____

Use rehearsal in conjunction with the above strategies. Encourage the student to write down the mnemonics and to say them out loud if possible.

Classroom Note Taking

It is important to take notes so that you have a permanent record of the information presented in class.

Concentrate or focus on what the teacher is saying. Identify the important points or ideas of the lecture and write them down. Try to relate the information to what you already know or to your interests.

If you do not understand what the teacher is saying, ask questions or ask for clarification. Write your question down if the teacher asks you to wait to ask questions at the end of the lecture. Confirm information if you have concerns about the information.

Keep your notes organized. Practice taking notes in an outline format. Highlight the main points in your notes.

Reorganize your notes after class if needed. Add examples or ideas you thought of during the lecture but did not have time to write down.

If allowed, bring a tape recorder to class and record the lecture. Take notes during the lecture. After class, replay the tape and check your notes to see if you missed any important information. Add the missed information to your notes as you review the recorded lecture.

Use mnemonic strategies and rehearsal to help you remember the information in your notes.

Understanding What You Have Read

1. Use the SQ3R method when reading textbooks, magazine articles, news articles, or any other lengthy reading material. The steps involved are as follows:

   S = **S**urvey the reading. Get an idea of what the material is about.

   Q = **Q**uestion. Ask yourself questions about the reading material. For example: Who is the story about? When did it happen? Where did it happen?

   R = **R**ead to answer your questions. Pay attention to underlined words and bold print.

   R = **R**ecite what you have read.

   R = **R**eview what you have read. Look back at the text to locate any details or main points you may have missed or forgotten.

2. Use a highlighter to mark main points or key words. Read the paragraph or section as a whole before going back to highlight the main points. If you read it first, it will be easier to identify what needs to be highlighted. Do not over-highlight. Just mark the important words or phrases.

3. Write down the main points and details after you have read a section of the chapter or article.

4. If you are reading a chapter or long article, break it up into smaller sections. Take breaks if needed.

5. Make sure it is quiet when you read. Turn off the TV, radio, and stereo. This will help you focus on your reading.

General Memory Techniques

Mnemonic strategies can be used to help you remember information. The basic strategies include:

Storytelling

Make up a story using the items on the list. It is easier to recall a story than a series of unrelated words, especially if you need to remember the words in a specific order.

Association

Associate the information you need to learn with something you already know.

Example: Station*e*ry that you write on has an "e" in it because you put it in an *e*nvelope.

First-Letter Association

Make up a word out of the first letters of the items you need to remember.

Example: *ROY G. BIV* stands for the colors of the rainbow— *r*ed, *o*range, *y*ellow, *g*reen, *b*lue, *i*ndigo, and *v*iolet.

Sentences can be made up to help remember how to spell a word.

Example: *Arithmetic*—"**A** *r*at *i*n *t*he *h*ouse *m*ight *e*at *t*he *i*ce *c*ream."

Visualization

Create a mental picture of a scene containing the items to be remembered. Draw the picture to help you remember it.

Rhyming

Make up a rhyme of the material you are trying to learn.

Example: In fourteen hundred and ninety-two, Columbus sailed the ocean blue.

(continued)

Face-Name Association

This is a variation of the visualization strategy. Make a visual association between the name and a distinctive feature of the person. Then draw a picture of the visual association.

Rehearsal and Relaxation

Rehearse the information and the mnemonic you are trying to remember. Overlearning material will increase your retrieval speed and improve your confidence. Relaxing will decrease mental blocks.

Always use rehearsal in conjunction with other strategies. If you have multiple lists of information to remember, make your mnemonics different to avoid confusion. Write down your lists and mnemonics as you rehearse them. Practice saying them aloud if possible.

Study Reminders Checklist

✔ Decrease distractions when you are studying. You need to be mentally alert when you study.

✔ Study each subject in separate study sessions.

✔ Space out your study sessions. Make your sessions one hour long or shorter.

✔ Begin studying far enough in advance so you are not forced to learn too much information at once.

✔ If you have a large amount of information to learn, break the information into parts. Learn the first part of the information, and then the second part. Review the first and second parts, and then move on to the third part. Review previously learned parts as a whole.

✔ Review the information you have learned out loud without looking at your notes or textbook. Look at your notes only if necessary.

✔ Use mnemonic strategies along with rehearsal.

✔ Use the SQ3R reading strategy for reading textbooks.

✔ Overlearning information will give you confidence and decrease anxiety during testing.

9 Memory Book Pages

- **Introductory Pages**
    Name Label
    Emergency Information Sheet
- **Schedules**
    Daily Schedules
    Weekly Schedules
- **References Pages — General**
    Table of Contents
    Personal Information
    Therapy Goals
    Chart for Filling Pill Organizer
    Medical History
    Medications
    Car Repair Record
    Telephone Messages
    Current News Issues
    Monthly Expenditures
    Bills
    Bus Schedules
    To Do Today
    Project Plan
    Grocery List
    Daily Meal Planner
    Weekly Meal Planner
    Telephone Numbers
    Photos of Important People
    Blank Reference Sheet
    Therapy Assignments

- **Reference Pages — School Age**
  - Class Project and Test Schedule
  - Personal Information
  - Daily Assignment Sheet
  - Class Schedule
  - Homework Time Management Sheet
  - Teacher/Parent Log
  - Directions to Classrooms
  - Classroom Policies
  - Behavioral Contract
  - Classroom Lecture
- **Notes**

Return this Book to:

Name: _____

Address: _____

_____

_____

Phone: _____

Return this Book to:

Name:_____

Address: _____

_____

Phone: _____

Emergency Information

Phone Numbers

Emergency:

Doctor:

Pharmacy:

Family:

My Address is:

My Phone Number is:

Emergency Information

Phone Numbers

Emergency:

Doctor:

Pharmacy:

Family:

My Address is:

My Phone Number is:

Daily Schedule

Today's Date:

Day of the Week:

Daily Schedule

Today's Date:

		To Do Today
8:00 A.M.		
8:30 A.M.		
9:00 A.M.		
9:30 A.M.		
10:00 A.M.		
10:30 A.M.		
11:00 A.M.		
11:30 A.M.		
12:00 Noon		
12:30 P.M.		
1:00 P.M.		
1:30 P.M.		
2:00 P.M.		
2:30 P.M.		
3:00 P.M.		
3:30 P.M.		
4:00 P.M.		
4:30 P.M.		

		To Do Today
5:00 P.M.		
5:30 P.M.		
6:00 P.M.		
6:30 P.M.		
7:00 P.M.		
7:30 P.M.		
8:00 P.M.		
8:30 P.M.		
9:00 P.M.		
9:30 P.M.		
10:00 P.M.		

Daily Schedule

Today's Date:

Time		
6:30 A.M.		
7:00 A.M.		
7:30 A.M.		
8:00 A.M.		
8:30 A.M.		
9:00 A.M.		
9:30 A.M.		
10:00 A.M.		
10:30 A.M.		
11:00 A.M.		
11:30 A.M.		
12:00 Noon		
12:30 P.M.		
1:00 P.M.		
1:30 P.M.		
2:00 P.M.		
2:30 P.M.		
3:00 P.M.		

3:30 P.M.		
4:00 P.M.		
4:30 P.M.		
5:00 P.M.		
5:30 P.M.		
6:00 P.M.		
6:30 P.M.		
7:00 P.M.		
7:30 P.M.		
8:00 P.M.		
8:30 P.M.		
9:00 P.M.		

_____

_____

_____

_____

_____

Weekly Schedule

Date: Monday	Date: Tuesday	Date: Wednesday	Date: Thursday	Date: Friday
8:00	8:00	8:00	8:00	8:00
8:30	8:30	8:30	8:30	8:30
9:00	9:00	9:00	9:00	9:00
9:30	9:30	9:30	9:30	9:30
10:00	10:00	10:00	10:00	10:00
10:30	10:30	10:30	10:30	10:30
11:00	11:00	11:00	11:00	11:00
11:30	11:30	11:30	11:30	11:30
12:00	12:00	12:00	12:00	12:00
12:30	12:30	12:30	12:30	12:30
1:00	1:00	1:00	1:00	1:00
1:30	1:30	1:30	1:30	1:30
2:00	2:00	2:00	2:00	2:00
2:30	2:30	2:30	2:30	2:30
3:00	3:00	3:00	3:00	3:00
3:30	3:30	3:30	3:30	3:30
4:00	4:00	4:00	4:00	4:00
4:30	4:30	4:30	4:30	4:30
5:00	5:00	5:00	5:00	5:00
5:30	5:30	5:30	5:30	5:30
6:00	6:00	6:00	6:00	6:00
To Do Today:	To Do Today:	To Do Today:	To Do Today:	To Do Today:

Weekly Schedule

| Date: Saturday | | Date: Sunday |

Saturday	Sunday
8:00	8:00
8:30	8:30
9:00	9:00
9:30	9:30
10:00	10:00
10:30	10:30
11:00	11:00
11:30	11:30
12:00	12:00
12:30	12:30
1:00	1:00
1:30	1:30
2:00	2:00
2:30	2:30
3:00	3:00
3:30	3:30
4:00	4:00
4:30	4:30
5:00	5:00
5:30	5:30
6:00	6:00
To Do Today:	To Do Today:

Month: _____

Sunday	Monday	Tuesday	Wednesday	Thursday	Friday	Saturday

Reference

Table of Contents

<u>Reference</u>

Table of Contents

Page 19 _____

Page 20 _____

Page 21 _____

Page 22 _____

Page 23 _____

Page 24 _____

Page 25 _____

Page 26 _____

Page 27 _____

Page 28 _____

Page 29 _____

Page 30 _____

Page 31 _____

Page 32 _____

Page 33 _____

Page 34 _____

Page 35 _____

Reference

Subject: Personal Information

Name: _____

Address: _____

_____

Phone number: _____

Age: _____

Date of birth: _____

Father's name: _____ **Age:** _____

Mother's name: _____ **Age:** _____

Names of children: _____ **Age:** _____

_____ **Age:** _____

_____ **Age:** _____

_____ **Age:** _____

Names of grandchildren:	**Parents:**	
_____		
_____		

Brother's name: _____

_____ **Age:** _____

_____ **Age:** _____

_____ **Age:** _____

_____ **Age:** _____

Sister's name:

_____ **Age:**

_____ **Age:**

_____ **Age:**

_____ **Age:**

Educational Background

School: **Dates attended:**

_____

_____

_____

Work History

Place of employment: **Dates employed:**

_____

_____

_____

Job responsibilities:

_____

_____

Hobbies

_____

_____

_____

_____

Other Personal Data:

_____

_____

_____

_____

_____

_____

_____

_____

_____

_____

_____

_____

_____

_____

_____

_____

_____

_____

_____

_____

_____

Reference

Subject: ┃Therapy Goals┃

Type of therapy: _____

Name of therapist: _____

Therapy goal: _____

Steps to reach goal: _____

_____

_____

_____

_____

Strategies to use each day: _____

_____

_____

_____

_____

Date Goal Reached: ┃ ┃

Reference

Chart for Filling Pill Organizer

	Sun.	Mon.	Tues.	Wed.	Thurs.	Fri.	Sat.
	Morning	Morning	Morning	Morning	Morning	Morning	Morning
	Noon	Noon	Noon	Noon	Noon	Noon	Noon
	Evening	Evening	Evening	Evening	Evening	Evening	Evening
	Bedtime	Bedtime	Bedtime	Bedtime	Bedtime	Bedtime	Bedtime

(Glue pills on sheet or write description of pills in the appropriate spaces. Color-coding squares may make it easier to read chart.)

Reference

Subject: Medical History

Type of injury:
_____

Date of injury:
_____

Dates of hospitalization:
_____

Name of hospital:
_____

Location of hospital:
_____

Surgeries:
_____

_____

Therapy received: **Therapists:**
_____

_____

_____

_____

_____

_____

Physicians:
_____

_____

Reference

Subject: Medications

Name of medication	Reason for taking medication	Dosage

If the following symptoms occur, contact your physician:

Reference

Car Repair Record

Date:

Odometer reading:

Maintenance performed:

Amount paid: $

Date:

Odometer reading:

Maintenance performed:

Amount paid: $

Date:

Odometer reading:

Maintenance performed:

Amount paid: $

Date:

Odometer reading:

Maintenance performed:

Amount paid: $

Date:

Odometer reading:

Maintenance performed:

Amount paid: $

Next Scheduled Service

Date:

Odometer:

Maintenance type:

Date:

Odometer:

Maintenance type:

Date:

Odometer:

Maintenance type:

Date:

Odometer:

Maintenance type:

Date:

Odometer:

Maintenance type:

Put the next scheduled service date on your calendar!

Telephone Messages

Date:	
Time:	
Who called:	
Message:	
Phone number:	

Date:	
Time:	
Who called:	
Message:	
Phone number:	

Date:	
Time:	
Who called:	
Message:	
Phone number:	

Current News Issues

Topic:

Where did the event take place?

What happened?

When did it happen?

List details:

Topic:

Where did the event take place?

What happened?

When did it happen?

List details:

Monthly Expenditures

Month _____

Date	Description of purchase	Amount of purchase	Balance

Bills

Month _____

Company	Date Received	Date Due	Date Paid	Amount Paid

Total Paid:

Reference

Subject: Bus Schedules

Destination	Bus stop
Bus number:	
Departure times	**Arrival times**
Important landmarks	

Destination	Bus stop
Bus number:	
Departure times	**Arrival times**
Important landmarks	

To Do Today

- [ ] 1 _____
- [ ] 2 _____
- [ ] 3 _____
- [ ] 4 _____
- [ ] 5 _____
- [ ] 6 _____
- [ ] 7 _____
- [ ] 8 _____
- [ ] 9 _____
- [ ] 10 _____
- [ ] 11 _____
- [ ] 12 _____
- [ ] 13 _____
- [ ] 14 _____
- [ ] 15 _____

Reference

Project Plan

Project:	
Things to purchase:	
Things to gather:	
Steps to complete task:	

1	
2	
3	
4	
5	
6	
7	
8	

Reference

Grocery List

Dairy		Produce		Canned Goods	
1		1		1	
2		2		2	
3		3		3	
4		4		4	
Meat/Fish		**Bakery/Breads**		**Beverages**	
1		1		1	
2		2		2	
3		3		3	
4		4		4	
Baking Supplies		**Cereal**		**Frozen Foods**	
1		1		1	
2		2		2	
3		3		3	
4		4		4	

(continued)

Deli		Chips/Crackers		Canned Goods	
1		1		1	
2		2		2	
3		3		3	
4		4		4	

Candy		Paper Products		Pet Supplies	
1		1		1	
2		2		2	
3		3		3	
4		4		4	

Detergents/Cleaners		Other		Other	
1		1		1	
2		2		2	
3		3		3	
4		4		4	

Daily Meal Planner

| Day of the Week: | | Date: | |

Breakfast Menu

Steps to complete the meal	
1	
2	
3	
4	
5	
6	
7	
8	
9	

Lunch Menu

Steps to complete the meal	
1	
2	
3	
4	
5	
6	
7	
8	
9	

Dinner Menu

Steps to complete the meal	
1	
2	
3	
4	
5	
6	
7	
8	
9	

Weekly Meal Planner

For the Week of:

Sunday	Things to buy:
Breakfast	
Lunch	
Dinner	

Monday	Things to buy:
Breakfast	
Lunch	
Dinner	

Tuesday	Things to buy:
Breakfast	
Lunch	
Dinner	

Wednesday	Things to buy:
Breakfast	
Lunch	
Dinner	

For the Week of:

Thursday	Things to buy:
Breakfast	
Lunch	
Dinner	

Friday	Things to buy:
Breakfast	
Lunch	
Dinner	

Saturday	Things to buy:
Breakfast	
Lunch	
Dinner	

Additional items to buy:

_____

_____

_____

_____

_____

Reference

Telephone Numbers

Name:

Address:

Phone Number:

Name:

Address:

Phone Number:

Name:

Address:

Phone Number:

Reference

Subject: Photos of Important People

Name:

Title:

Describe how you could associate this person's name, face, and title.

_____

_____

_____

_____

<u>Reference</u>

Subject: [   ]

_____

_____

_____

_____

_____

_____

_____

_____

_____

_____

_____

_____

Reference

Therapy Assignments

Date Given	Assignment	Due Date

Class Project and Test Schedule

Month: _____

Locker number: _____

Locker combination: _____

Monday	Tuesday	Wednesday	Thursday	Friday

Reference

Subject: Personal Information

Name: _____

Address: _____

_____

Phone number: _____

Age: _____

Date of birth: _____

Father's name: _____ **Age:** _____

Mother's name: _____ **Age:** _____

Father's work place: _____ **Phone:** _____

Mother's work place: _____ **Phone:** _____

Brother's name: _____

_____ **Age:** _____

_____ **Age:** _____

_____ **Age:** _____

_____ **Age:** _____

Sister's name: _____

_____ **Age:** _____

_____ **Age:** _____

_____ **Age:** _____

_____ **Age:** _____

(continued)

Emergency contact: _____

Name: _____

Address: _____

_____

Phone: _____

_____

School currently attending: _____

Address: _____

_____

Phone: _____

_____

Principal: _____

Teachers' names: _____

_____

_____

_____

_____

Health insurance company: _____

_____

Physician: _____

_____

Phone: _____

Daily Assignment Sheet

Date Given	Assignment	Date Due	Teacher's initials	Parent's initials	Grade received

Class Schedule

Period 1:

Class:

Teacher:

Room number:

Location:

Period 5:

Class:

Teacher:

Room number:

Location:

Period 2:

Class:

Teacher:

Room number:

Location:

Period 6:

Class:

Teacher:

Room number:

Location:

Period 3:

Class:

Teacher:

Room number:

Location:

Period 7:

Class:

Teacher:

Room number:

Location:

Period 4:

Class:

Teacher:

Room number:

Location:

Period 8:

Class:

Teacher:

Room number:

Location:

Homework Time Management Sheet

Class:	Class time:
Teacher:	Room number:

Homework assignments to be completed	Date due:
1	
2	
3	
4	
5	
6	
7	
8	
9	
10	

Order in which to work on assignments

1	
2	
3	
4	
5	
6	
7	
8	
9	
10	

Work schedule

:	to	:	work on
:	to	:	work on
:	to	:	work on
:	to	:	work on
:	to	:	work on
:	to	:	work on
:	to	:	work on

© 1994 by Communication Skill Builders, Inc. / 602-323-7500 / This page may be reproduced for instructional use. / Catalog No. 3041

Teacher/Parent Log

Date	Teacher's notes to parent

_____
_____
_____
_____
_____
_____
_____
_____
_____
_____
_____

Date	Parent's notes to teachers

_____
_____
_____
_____
_____
_____
_____
_____
_____
_____
_____
_____
_____

Date	Permission slip needed for:	Sign and return by:

_____
_____
_____

The following library books are due:	Date due:

_____
_____
_____
_____
_____

Directions to Classrooms

Period:

Class:

Room number:

Directions:

Period:

Class:

Room number:

Directions:

Period:

Class:

Room number:

Directions:

Period:

Class:

Room number:

Directions:

Place map here:

Classroom Policies

Class:	Class time:
Teacher:	Room number:

Classroom policies:

1 _____

_____

2 _____

_____

3 _____

_____

4 _____

_____

5 _____

_____

6 _____

_____

7 _____

_____

8 _____

_____

9 _____

_____

10 _____

_____

Grading policy:

_____

_____

_____

Class supplies:

_____

_____

_____

Behavioral Contract

Problem:

Goal:

I, _____, agree to the following terms:

I will _____

I will _____

I will _____

I will _____

I will _____

I will _____

Parent/teacher will

_____

_____

_____   _____

Signature   **Date**

_____   _____

Signature   **Date**

Classroom Lecture

Class: _____   **Teacher:** _____

                                        Date: _____

Topic:

Main point:

Details:

Examples:

Questions:

Main point:

Details:

Examples:

Questions:

Notes

10 Environmental Cues

Introduction

Placing visual cues to the environment can help some cognitively impaired patients complete daily tasks more independently. Calendars, emergency phone numbers, cupboard labels, and written directions are all examples of visual cues that can be placed in the home. The clinician should identify the problems that the patient is experiencing in the home environment and establish visual cues to help the patient compensate for those problems.

Environmental cue stickers can be used to mark doors, cupboards, and dressers to assist patients in locating rooms in the house and items in the rooms. Marking doors using word and picture labels can assist some patients with pathfinding in the home. This strategy can be especially helpful for some patients who exhibit wandering/searching behaviors. The picture and word label helps the patient quickly identify where each room is located.

basement

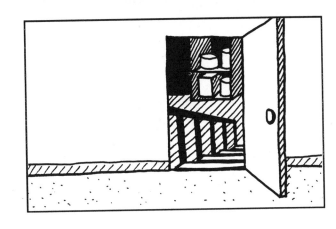

bathroom

bedroom

bills

bowls

canned food

cleaners

closet

cups

garage

garbage

glasses

glasses

hairbrush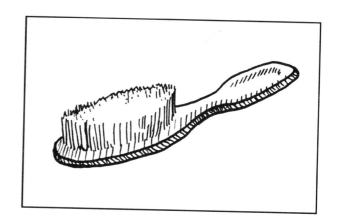

hearing aid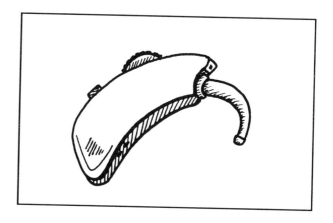

jewelry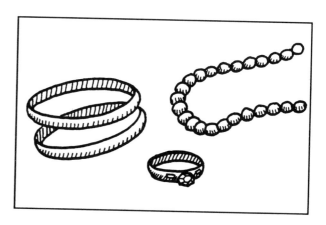

keys

kitchen

laundry room

living room

medicine

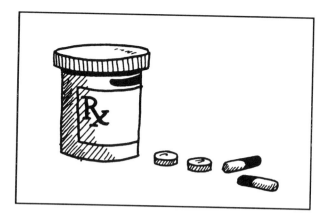

money

pans

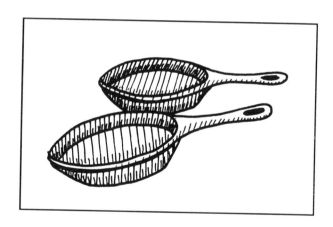

pantry

pants

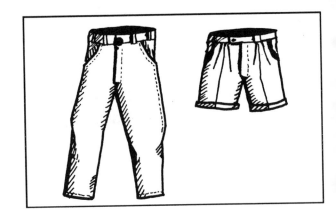

pencils

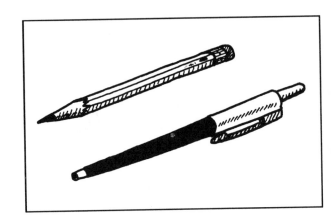

plates

pots

purse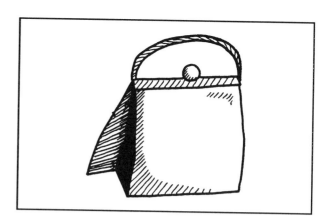

shirts

shoes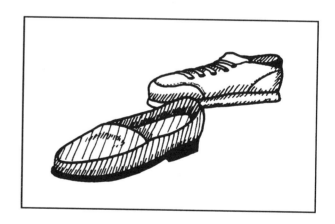

silverware

socks

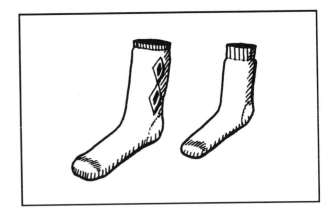

spices

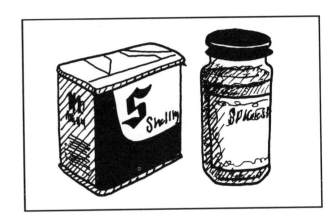

Stop.
Do not enter.

sweaters

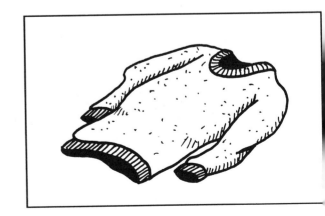

toothbrush
and
toothpaste

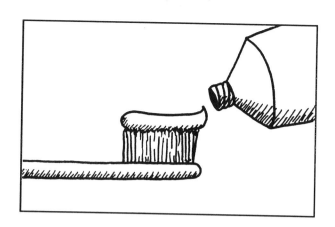

towels

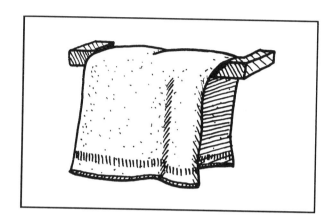

underwear

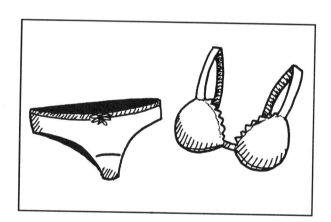

underwear

Safety Checklist

✔___ Turn down heat/air conditioner

✔___ Turn off stove/oven

✔___ Turn off lights

✔___ Turn iron off

✔___ Turn off electric blanket

✔___ Turn off stereo

✔___ Close windows

✔___ Turn on answering machine

✔___ Take house keys

✔___ Take your wallet/purse

✔___ Check for I.D. in wallet/purse

✔___ Take your watch

✔___ Take your memory book

Appendices

A. **Commercial External Memory Aids**

B. **Examples of Completed Memory Book Pages**

Appendix A
Commercial External Memory Aids

With technology changing so rapidly, the availability of commercial memory aids is also constantly changing. As new systems are updated, old models are discontinued. The following are a few of the systems currently on the market. Check with your local electronics store to determine what systems are available in your area. Before purchasing, put the system through its paces: try storing and retrieving some information to determine how easy it is to use the system.

Electronic Organizers

Systems with Alarm Features

Sharp Wizard 512KB OZ-9600II
Top-of-the-line electronic organizer
"QWERTY" style keyboard
40-character x eight-line display
Basic functions plus many business features
Approximate price: **$500**

Sharp Wizard OZ-8200
128K memory
Same basic features as the OZ-8000
Approximate price: **$399**

The Wizard systems have larger keys and screens compared to other organizers. Numerous steps are involved in storing and retrieving information in the system. Sharp manufactures a printer and cassette interface that can be used with all Wizard organizers (Sharp CE 50 P).

Casio Electronic Organizer SF-8000
64KB memory capacity
32 columns with six-line display
Calendar, memo, and telephone directory function
Approximate price: **$200**

Casio SF 4300 Electronic Organizer
32KB memory
1500 telephone number capacity
Schedule system, full month calendar, memory and
letter memory functions
Approximate price: **$120**

Royal Personal Organizer DM220 Electronic Organizer
66KB memory
Telephone list, memo function, scheduler, business card file
Screen is smaller than the Wizard
Approximate price: **$190**

Texas Instruments TI-PS 3600
Data bank
8KB memory
Three-line display with 12 characters per line
"QWERTY" type
Clock in system
Approximate price: **$40**

Inexpensive Organizers without Alarm

Seiko Instruments SII Student Organizer
Seiko Instruments DF 3000 Shopping Organizer
Seiko Instruments DF 3400 Personal Organizer
Letters are difficult to read on the screen; the screen is small
Approximate price: **$20**

These are just a few of the electronic organizers that are currently on the market. Most office supply stores carry a wide variety of systems .In general, the systems are complicated to use and require good fine motor skills and vision. Even individuals without brain injury find it difficult to remember how to store and retrieve information from the systems.

Notebook-Style Personal Organizers

The following is a list of several companies that manufacture personal organizers. Most office supply stores carry several different systems.

Design House, Inc.
185 W. Englewood Ave.
Teaneck, NJ 07666-3526

Super Trax
Southworth Company
West Springfield, MA 01090

Day Runner Personal Organizers
Day Runner, Inc.
Fullerton, CA 92633

Day-Timers, Inc.
One Day-Timer Plaza
Allentown, PA 18195-1551

Rolodex Corporation
245 Secaucus Road
Secaucus, NJ 07094-2196

Other Commercial Aids

Home Activity Center (#23335-00)
Contains a large vinyl holder (17" x 20"), large refillable ruled monthly calendar, schedule grids, full yearly overview calendar on each page, birthday and special date cards, important telephone cards, and refillable note pads.
Approximate price: **$20**

Manufacturer:
Design House, Inc.
185 W. Englewood Ave
Teaneck, NJ 07666-3526

Medication Alarms/Electronic Pill Timers

Quartz electronic pill timer can be set from 1 minute to 24 hours. The alarm is automatic and will repeat alarm at the programmed intervals.

Manufacturer:
Bruce Medical Supply
Stock No. BMS507
411 Waverly Oaks Rd.
P.O. Box 9166
Waltham, MA 02254

Other Alarm Systems

Casio manufactures a number of wristwatch alarm systems. Casio has a publication, *Wrist Technology*, that describes its product titles. You can obtain a copy of this publication by writing to:

Casio
570 Mt. Pleasant Avenue
P.O. Box 7000
Dover, NJ 07801

Pager Systems

Pagers can be used as a reminder system to alert patients of appointments, medication schedules, job tasks, social events, and so forth. Paging systems can help patients manage their time on the job and can help remind them to complete daily and weekly tasks until the these eventually become habit. Many pagers have oversized displays that are easy to read.

NEC Facts Provider Pager
This alphanumeric pager has an oversized display screen
that can display up to four lines of text (80 letters and numbers).
It has a built-in clock, automatic screen illumination,
and factory- and user-defined messages. An electronic
calendar can be programmed, with the alarm sounding
at predetermined times.

For more information on the pager, write:
NEC America, Inc.
383 Omni Dr.
Richardson, TX 75080

There are numerous paging systems and dispatch services available. Look in the Yellow Pages of your telephone directory under "Paging" for information in your area. McCaw Cellular Communications Company has a nationwide paging service and can be reached at 1-800-562-2337 for more information about its services.

Appendix B

Examples of Completed Memory Book Pages

Daily Schedule

Today's Date: December 20, 1994

Day of the Week: Tuesday

9:00

Breakfast - I had pancakes and orange juice.

9:30

Speech therapy with Linda. Worked on slowing down my speech rate. I was able to identify all 4 sections of my memory book.

10:00

Occupational therapy with Teresa. I made cookies. I used a checklist when cooking to help with organization. (It is in my "reference section".)

10:30

Break - I watched a game show on T.V. I started to write a letter to a friend.

11:00

Memory Group - worked on recording information in my memory book.

Reference

Project Plan

Project: Making Cookies	

Things to purchase: Eggs, butter and sugar

Things to gather: Measuring cups, spoons, mixing bowls, cookie sheet, mixer, eggs, butter, flour, sugar (brown and white)

Steps to complete task:

✔ 1		Go shopping + buy eggs. butter + sugar
✔ 2		Gather above items + turn on oven to 350°
✔ 3		Measure sugar + flour in a bowl.
✔ 4		Add eggs and butter; Mix
✔ 5		Spoon onto ungreased cookie sheet
6		Bake cookies at 350° for 12 mins.
7		Cool cookies on a rack
8		Clean up

Behavioral Contract

Problem: | I am late to class.
| |
| |

Goal: | I will be on time to class and will bring all
| of my materials for 2 weeks.
| |

I, _____Jim Bow_____, **agree to the following terms:**

I will be in the classroom ready to work when the
second bell rings.

I will bring a pencil, pen, paper, and notebook to
class each day.

I will bring my completed work assignments
to class each day.

I will _____

I will _____

I will _____

Parent/(teacher) will

mark in my book each day I complete my goal,
schedule 30 mins. of gametime on the computer when
I reach my goal.

_____Jim Bow_____   _____Sept. 19, 1994_____
Signature   **Date**

_____Linda Swain_____   _____Sept. 19, 1994_____
Signature   **Date**

References

Albert, M. L., N. Butters, and J. Brandt. 1981. Patterns of remote memory in amnesic and demented patients. *Archives of Neurology* 38:495-500.

Anschutz, L., C. J. Camp, R. P. Markley, and J. J. Kramer. 1985. Maintenance and generalization of mnemonics for grocery shopping by older adults. *Experimental Aging Research* 11:157-60.

Atkinson, R. C., and R. M. Shiffrin. 1968. Human memory: A proposed system and its control processes. In *Psychology of learning and motivation: Advances in research and theory*, edited by K. W. Spence and J. T. Spence, 89-195. New York: Academic Press.

Baddeley, A. D., and E. K. Warrington. 1973. Memory coding and amnesia. *Neuropsychologia 11:159-65.*

Batt, R., and P. Lounsbury. 1990. Teaching the patient with cognitive deficits to use a computer. *American Journal of Occupational Therapy* 11 (Apr):361-67.

Botwinick, J., and M. Storandt. 1974. *Memory for span and sequential patterns: Memory related function and age.* Springfield, IL: Charles C. Thomas.

Bourgeois, M. 1992. Evaluating memory wallets in conversations with persons with dementia. *Journal of Speech and Hearing Research* 35 (Dec):1344-57.

Bower, G. H., and J. S. Reitman. 1972. Mnemonic elaboration in multi-list learning. *Journal of Verbal Learning and Visual Behavior* 11:478-85.

Brooks, D. N. 1976. Wechsler Memory Scale performance and its relationship to brain damage after severe closed head injury. *Journal of Neurology, Neurosurgery and Psychiatry* 39:593.

————. 1980. Cognitive sequelae in relationship to early indices of severity of brain damage after severe blunt head injury. *Journal of Neurology, Neurosurgery and Psychiatry* 52:611-24.

Brooks, D. N., and A. D. Baddeley. 1976. What can amnesics learn? *Neuropsychologia* 14:111-22.

Brookshire, R. H. 1978. *An introduction to aphasia.* Minneapolis, MN: BRK.

Buell, S., and P. Coleman. 1979. Dentritic growth in the aged human brain and failure of growth in senile dementia. *Science* 206:854-55.

Bugelski, B. R. 1977. The association of images. In *Images, perception, and knowledge*, edited by J. M. Nichols, 37-46. Boston: D. Reidel.

Butters, N., M. Albert, and D. Sax. 1979. Investigations of the memory disorders of patients with Huntington's disease. *Advances in Neurology* 23:203-12.

Capruso, D., and H. Levin. 1992. Cognitive impairment following closed head injury. *Neurologic Clinics.* 10 (Nov):879-93.

Carr, J. 1980. Imitation, discrimination and generalization. In *Behavior modification for the mentally handicapped*, edited by W. Yule and J. Carr, 79-89. London: Croom Helm.

Cave, C. B., and L. R. Squire. 1992. Intact verbal and nonverbal short-term memory following damage to the human hippocampus. *Hippocampus* 2:151-63.

Cermak, L. S. 1975. Imagery, an aid to retrieval for Korsakoff patients. *Cortex* 11:163-69.

Ciocon, J., and J. Potter. 1988. Age related changes in human memory: Normal and abnormal. *Geriatrics* 43 (Oct):43-48.

Clark, L., and J. Knowles. 1973. Age differences in dichotic listening performance. *Journal of Gerontology* 28:173-78.

Colwell, S. 1984. The adolescent with developmental disorders. In *Chronic illness and disabilities in childhood and adolescence*, edited by R. Blum, 327-46. Orlando, FL: Grune & Stratton.

Craik, F. I. 1968. Short term memory and the aging process. In *Human aging and behavior*, edited by G. A. Talland, 131-168. New York: Academic Press.

_____. 1977. Age differences in human memory. In *Human aging and behavior*, edited by J. Birren and K. Schaie, 384-420. New York: Van Nostrand Reinhold.

Craik, F. I. M. 1979. Conclusions and comments. In *Levels of processing in human memory*, edited by L. S. Cermak and F. I. M. Craik, 197-222. Hillsdale, NJ: Erlbaum.

_____. 1985. Paradigms in human memory research. In *Perspectives on learning and memory*, edited by L. Nilsson and T. Archer, 200. Hillsdale, NJ: Erlbaum.

Crovitz, H. F. 1979. Memory retraining in brain-damaged patients: The airplane list. *Cortex* 15:131-34.

Cummings, J. L., D. F. Benson, M. J. Walsh, and H. L. Levine. 1979. Left-to-right transfer of language dominance: A case study. *Neurology* 29:1547-50.

Deffenbacher, J. L., and S. L. Hazaleus. 1985. Cognitive, emotional and physiological components of test anxiety. *Cognitive Therapy and Research* 9:69-80.

Devor, M. 1982. Plasticity in the adult nervous system. In *Rehabilitation of the neurological patient*, edited by L. S. Illis, E. M. Sedgwick, and H. T. Glanville, 44-84. Oxford: Blackwell Scientific Publications.

Elliot, J. L., and J. R. Gentile. 1986. The efficacy of a mnemonic technique for learning disabled and non-disabled adolescents. *Journal of Learning Disabilities* 19:237-41.

Ericsson, K. A., W. G. Chase, and S. Falcon. 1980. Acquisition of a memory skill. *Science* 208:1181-82.

Eson, M., J. Yen, and R. Bourke. 1978. Assessment of recovery from serious head injury. *Journal of Neurology, Neurosurgery and Psychiatry* 41:1036.

Gianutsos, R., and B. B. Grynbaum. 1983. Helping brain-injured people to contend with hidden cognitive deficits. *International Rehabilitation Medicine* 5:37-40.

Giles, G., and M. Shore. 1989. The effectiveness of an electronic memory aid for a memory-impaired adult of normal intelligence. *American Journal of Occupational Therapy* 43 (Jun):409-11.

Ginn, H. 1975. Neurobehavioral dysfunction in uremia. *Kidney International* 217(2):217-21.

Gittleman-Klein, R., S. Manuzze, R. Skenker, and N. Bonagura. 1985. Hyperactive boys almost grown up. *Archives of General Psychiatry* 42:937-47.

Glanze, W., K. Anderson, and L. Anderson. 1985. *Mosby medical encyclopedia*. 2d ed. New York: Penguin.

Glanzer, M., and A. R. Cunitz. 1966. Two storage mechanisms in free recall. *Journal of Verbal Learning and Verbal Behavior* 5:351-60.

Glasgow, R. E., R. A. Zeiss, M. Barrera, and P. M. Lewinsohn. 1977. Case studies on remediating memory deficits in brain damaged individuals. *Journal of Clinical Psychology* 33:1049-54.

Glees, P., and J. Cole. 1950. Recovery of skilled motor functions after small repeated lesions of motor cortex in macaques. *Journal of Neurophysiology* 13:137-48.

Glisky, E., and D. Schacter. 1986. Remediation of organic memory disorders: Current status and future prospects. *Journal of Head and Trauma Rehabilitation* vol. 1 (Mar):1-96.

Godfrey, H., and R. Knight. 1985. Cognitive rehabilitation of memory functioning in amnesic alcoholics. *Journal of Consulting and Clinical Psychology* 53:555-57.

Golden, G. 1992. Attention deficit hyperactivity disorder. In *Child and adolescent neurology for psychiatrists*, edited by D. Kaufman, G. Solomon, and C. Pfeffer, 43-55. New York: Williams and Wilkins.

Gordon, T. E., P. Gordon, E. Valentine, and J. Wilding. 1984. One man's memory: A study of a mnemonist. *British Journal of Psychology* 72:1-14.

Grafman, J. 1984. Memory assessment and remediation. In *Behavioral assessment and rehabilitation of the traumatically brain-damaged*, edited by B. A. Edelstein and E. T. Couture, 151-86. New York: Plenum Press.

Groninger, L. D. 1971. Mnemonic imagery and forgetting. *Psychonomic Science* 23:161-3.

Grundman, M., M. Felder, H. Donnenfeld, and J. Masdeu. 1989. Neurology in AIDS. In *AIDS and infections of homosexual men*, edited by P. Ma and D. Armstrong, 265-280. Boston, MA: Butterworths.

Grunthal, E. 1947. Ueber das klinische Bild nach umschriebenem beiderseitigem Ausfall der Ammonshornrinde. *Monatschrift fur Psychaitrie und Neurologie* 113:1-16.

Guthrie, A., A. Presley, C. Greekie, and C. MacKenzie. 1980. The effects of alcohol on memory. In *Psychopharmacology of alcohol*, edited by M. Sandler, 79-88. New York: Grune and Stratton.

Harris, J. 1984. Methods of improving memory. In *Clinical management of memory problems*, edited by B. Wilson and N. J. Moffat, 46-63. Rockville, MD: Aspen.

Harris, J. E. 1980. Memory aids people use: Two interview studies. *Memory and Cognition* 8:31-8.

Harris, J. E., and A. Sunderland. 1981. A brief survey of the management of memory disorders in rehabilitation units. *Britain International Rehabilitation Medicine* 3:206-9.

Haynes, C. D., D. A. Gideon, G. D. King, and R. Dempsey. 1976. The improvement of cognition and personality after carotid enartrectomy. *Surgery* 80:699-704.

Hellebusch, S. J. 1976. Improving learning and memory in the aged: The effects of mnemonics on strategy, transfer and generalization. Ph.D. diss. abstract (1459-B Order No. 76-19, 496), University of Notre Dame.

Higbee, K. 1977a. Mental filing systems: Loci mnemonics. In *Your memory: How it works and how to improve it*, 144-56. New York: Paragon House.

————. 1977b. Working miracles with your memory: An introduction to mnemonics. In *Your memory: How it works and how to improve it*, 93-113. New York: Paragon House.

————. 1988. Working miracles with your memory: An introduction to mnemonics. In *Your memory: How it works and how to improve it*, 93-112. New York: Prentice Hall.

Hill, R. D., K. D. Evankovich, J. I. Sheikh, and J. A. Yesavage. 1987. Imagery mnemonic training in a patient with primary degenerative dementia. *Psychology and Aging* 2:204-05.

Jackson, H., and N. J. Moffat. 1983. Training motor coding with the severely head injured. Unpublished manuscript.

Johnston, L., and S. H. Gueldner. 1989. Remember when . . .? Using mnemonics to boost memory in the elderly. *Journal of Gerontology and Nursing* 15 (Aug):22-26.

Karlsberk, W. D. 1980. The national head and spinal cord injury survey: Major findings. *Journal of Neurology* 53:519.

Kelly, H. P. 1964. Memory abilities: A factor analysis. *Psychological Monogram* Vol. 2.

Khan, A. U. 1986. *Clinical disorders of memory.* New York: Plenum Medical Book Company.

Kra, S. 1986. *Aging myths: Reversible causes of mind and memory loss.* New York: McGraw-Hill.

Krop, H. D., A. J. Block, and E. Cohn. 1973. Neuropsychologic effects of continuous oxygen therapy in chronic obstructive pulmonary disease. *Chest* 64:317-22.

Lam, C., D. Priddy, and P. Johnson. 1991. *Rehabilitation Counseling Bulletin* 35 (Sept):68-74.

Lederman, R. J., and C. E. Henry. 1978. Progressive dialysis encephalopathy. *Annals of Neurology* 4:199-204.

Leng, N., and A. Copello. 1990. Rehabilitation of memory after brain injury: Is there an effective technique? *Clinical Rehabilitation* 4 (Feb):63-69.

Levine, M. D., R. Brooks, and J. P. Shonkoff. 1980. *A pediatric approach to learning disorders.* New York: John Wiley.

Lezak, M. D. 1979. Recovery of memory and learning functions following traumatic brain injury. *Cortex* 15:63-72.

Mason, S. E., and A. D. Smith. 1977. Imagery in the aged. *Experimental Aging Research* 3:17-32.

Mastropieri, M., T. Scruggs, and J. R. Levin. [1987] Mnemonic instruction in special education. In *Imagery and related mnemonic processes: Theories, individual differences, and applications*, edited by M. McDaniel and M. Pressley, 358-76. New York: Springer-Verlag.

Mateer, C. A., M. M. Sohlberg, and J. Crinean. 1987. Perceptions of memory function in individuals with closed-head injury. *Journal of Head and Trauma Rehabilitation* 2 (Sept):74-84.

McCough, G. P., G. M. Austin, C. N. Liu, and C. Y. Liu. 1958. Sprouting as a cause of spasticity. *Journal of Neurophysiology* 21:205-16.

Milner, B., S. Corkin, and J. L. Teuber. 1968. Further analysis of the hippocampal amnesic syndrome: A 14-year follow-up study of H.M. *Neuropsychologia* 6:215-34.

Milton, S. 1985. Compensatory strategy training: A practical approach for managing persisting memory problems. *Cognitive Rehabilitation* 3 (Nov-Dec):8-16.

Moely, B. E., and W. E. Jeffrey. 1974. The effect of organization training on children's free recall of category items. *Child Development* 45:135-43.

Moffat, N. 1984. Strategies for memory therapy. In *Clinical management of memory problems*, edited by B. Wilson and M. J. Moffat, 63-88. London: Croom Helm.

Moffat, N. J., and A. Coward. 1983. Training visual imagery for names with the head injured. Unpublished manuscript.

Morris, P. E., and R. L. Reid. 1970. The repeated use of mnemonic imagery. *Psychomonic Science* 20:337-38.

Morris, P. E., S. Jones, and P. Hampson. 1978. An imagery mnemonic for the learning of people's names. *British Journal of Psychology* 69:335-36.

Myers, J. L., K. Pezdek, and K. Coulson. 1973. Effect of prose organization upon free recall. *Journal of Educational Psychology* 65:313-20.

Nelson, R. J., A. Lonesio, P. Shimamura, R. F. Landwehr, and L. Narens. 1982. Overlearning and the feeling of knowing. *Journal of Experimental Psychology: Learning, Memory and Cognition* 8:279-88.

Paivio, A. 1983. Strategies in language learning. In *Cognitive strategy research: Educational applications*, edited by M. Pressley and J. R. Levin, 189-210. New York: Springer-Verlag.

Palmer, S. E. 1975. The effects of contextual scenes on the identification of objects. *Memory and Cognition* 3:519-26.

Patten, B. M. 1972. The ancient art of memory. *Archives of Neurology* 26:25-31.

Patton, G. W. R. 1986. The effect of the phonetic mnemonic system on memory for numerical material. *Human Learning* 5:21-28.

Penfield, W., and B. Milner. 1958. Memory deficit produced by bilateral lesions in the hippocampal zone. *A.M.A. Archives of Neurology and Psychiatry* 79:475-97.

Petro, S., D. Herrmann, D. Burrows, and C. Moore. 1991. Usefulness of commercial memory aids as a function of age. *International Journal of Aging and Human Development* 33:295-309.

Poon, L. W. 1985. Differences in human memory with aging: Nature, causes, and clinical applications. In *Handbook of the psychology of aging*. 2d ed., edited by J. E. Birren and K. W. Schaie, 427-62. New York: Van Nostrand Reinhold.

Postman, L. 1975. Verbal learning and memory. In *Annual review of psychology*, edited by M. R. Rosenzweig and L. W. Porter, 26. Palo Alto, CA: Annual Reviews.

Reason, J., and D. Lucas. 1984. Using cognitive diaries to investigate naturally occurring memory blocks. In *Everyday memory, actions, and absent-mindedness*, edited by J. E. Harris and P. E. Morris, 53-70. London: Academic Press.

Reigeluth, C. M. 1983. Meaningfulness and instruction: Relating what is being learned to what a student knows. *Instructional Science* 12:197-218.

Reisberg, B., S. Ferris, M. de Leon, and T. Crook. 1982. The global deterioration scale for assessment of primary degenerative dementia. *American Journal of Psychiatry* 139:1136-39.

Reitman, J. 1971. Mechanisms of forgetting in short-term memory. *Cognitive Psychology* 2:185-95.

Robbins, L., and D. Vinson. 1960. Objective psychological assessment of the thyrotoxic patient and response to treatment: Preliminary report. *Journal of Clinical Endocrinology* 20:120-29.

Robertson-Tchabo, E. A., C. P. Hausman, and D. Arenberg. 1976. A classical mnemonic for older learners: A trip that works. *Educational Gerontology* 1:215-26.

Robinson, F. B. 1970. *Effective study*. New York: Harper and Row.

Roediger, H. L. 1980. The effectiveness of four mnemonics in ordering recall. *Journal of Experimental Psychology: Human Learning and Memory* 6:558-67.

Rosenblum, M. L., R. M. Levy, and D. E. Bredesen. 1988. Central nervous system dysfunction in acquired immunodeficiency syndrome. In *AIDS and the nervous system*, edited by M. L. Rosenblum, R. M. Levy, and D. E. Bredesen, 29-63. New York: Raven Press.

Safer, D. J., and J. M. Krager. 1988. A survey of medication treatment for hyperactive/inattentive students. *Journal of American Medical Association* 260:2256.

Schacter, D., S. Rich, and A. Stamp. 1985. Remediation of memory disorders: Experimental evaluation of the spaced-retrieval technique. *Journal of Clinical and Experimental Neuropsychology* 7 (Feb):79-96.

Schon, M., A. Sutherland, and R. Rawson. 1961. The psychological effects of thyroid deficiency. In *Proceedings of 3rd World Congress in Psychiatry*. Montreal: McGill University Press.

Schonfield, D., and L. Wenger. 1975. Age limitation of perceptual span. *Nature* 253:377-78.

Scoville, W. B., and B. Milner. 1957. Loss of recent memory after bilateral hippocampal lesions. *Journal of Neurology, Neurosurgery and Psychiatry* 20:11-21.

Sell, S. H. 1983. Long term sequelae of bacterial meningitis in children. *Pediatric Infectious Diseases* 2:90-93.

Shallice, T., and E. K. Warrington. 1970. Independent functioning of verbal memory stores: A neuropsychological study. *Quarterly Journal of Experimental Psychology* 22:261-73.

Shiffrin, R. M., and W. Schneider. 1977. Controlled and automatic human information processing: II. Perceptual learning, automatic attending and a general theory. *Psychological Review* 84:127-90.

Simma, K. 1955. Die psychischen storungen bei lasionen des temporallappens und ihre Behandlung. *Monatschrift fur Psychaitrie und Neurologie* 13:130-60.

Slak, S. 1971. Long-term retention of random sequence digital information with the aid of phonemic recoding: A case report. *Perceptual and Motor Skills* 33:455-60.

Smith, A. D. 1975. Interaction between human aging and memory. *Georgia Institute of Technology Progress Report*, no. 2.

Sohlberg, M., and C. Mateer. 1989. Training use of compensatory memory books: A three stage behavioral approach. *Journal of Clinical and Experimental Neuropsychology* 11 (Dec):871-91.

Summerskill, W., E. Davidson, and S. Sherlock. 1956. Neuropsychiatric syndrome associated with hepatic cirrhosis and extensive portal collateral circulation. *Quarterly Journal of Medicine* 25:245-66.

Taub, H. 1973. Memory span, practice and aging. *Journal of Gerontology* 28:335-38.

Teasdale, G., and B. Jennett. 1974. Assessment of coma and impaired consciousness: A practical scale. *Lancet* 2:81.

Terry, R., A. Peck, R. DeTeresa, R. Schechter, and D. Horoupian. 1981. Some morphometric aspects of the brain in senile dementia of the Alzheimer type. *Annals of Neurology* 10:184-92.

Timme, V., D. Deyloff, M. Rogers, D. Dinnel, and J. A. Glover. 1986 (April). Oral directions: Remembering what to do when. Paper presented at meeting of American Educational Research Association, San Francisco.

Tulving, E. 1972. Episodic and semantic memory. In *Organization of memory*, edited by E. Tulving and W. Donaldson, 382-403. New York: Academic Press.

Walsh, S., and L. Thompson. 1978. Age differences in visual sensory memory. *Journal of Gerontology* 33:282-87.

Wehman, P., J. Kreutzer, P. Sale, M. West, M. V. Morton, and J. Diambra. 1989. Cognitive impairment and remediation: Implications for employment following traumatic brain injury. *Journal of Head and Trauma Rehabilitation* 4 (Sept):66-75.

Weiss, G., and L. Hechtman. 1985. The psychiatric status of hyperactives: A controlled prospective 15 year follow-up of 63 hyperactive children. *Journal of American Academic Child and Adolescent Psychiatry* 24:211-21.

Whybrow, P., A. Prange, and C. Treadway. 1969. Mental changes accompanying thyroid gland dysfunction. *Archives of General Psychiatry* 20:48-63.

Wickelgren, W. A. 1981. Human learning and memory. *Annual Review of Psychiatry*, edited by M. R. Rosenzweig and L. W. Porter, 32:21-57.

Williams, M., and J. Pennybacker. 1954. Memory disturbances in third ventricle tumors. *Journal of Neurology, Neurosurgery and Psychiatry* 17:115-23.

Wilson, B. 1981. Teaching a patient to remember people's names after removal of a left temporal tumor. *Behavioral Psychotherapy* 9:338-44.

———. 1982. Success and failure in memory training following a cerebral vascular accident. *Cortex* 18:581-94.

———. 1984. Memory therapy in practice. In *Clinical management of memory problems*, edited by B. Wilson and M. J. Moffat, 89-111. London: Croom Helm.

———. 1987a. A comparison of four mnemonic strategies in brain-damaged and non-brain-damaged subjects. In *Rehabilitation of memory*, edited by B. Wilson, 207-32. New York: Guilford Press.

———. 1987b. Cognitive psychology. In *Rehabilitation of memory*, edited by B. Wilson, 42-47. New York: Guilford Press.

———. 1987c. Investigations of the PQRST strategy for increasing recall of prose passages, In *Rehabilitation of memory*, edited by B. Wilson, 171-53. New York: Guilford Press.

———. 1987d. Using visual imagery for learning names. In *Rehabilitation of Memory*, edited by B. Wilson, 119-30. New York: Guilford Press.

———. 1987e. Visual imagery as a mnemonic aid for brain-damaged adults: A group study. In *Rehabilitation of Memory*, edited by B. Wilson, 4195-206. New York: Guilford Press.

———. 1992. Recovery and compensatory strategies in head injured memory impaired people several years after insult. *Journal of Neurology, Neurosurgery and Psychiatry* 55:177-80.

Wilson, B., and N. Moffat. 1984a. Running a memory group. In *Clinical Management of Memory Problems*, edited by B. A. Wilson and N. Moffat, 171-98. London: Croom Helm.

———. 1984b. Rehabilitation of memory for everyday life. In *Everyday memory: Actions and absent-mindedness*, edited by J. Harris and P. Morris, 207-32. London: Academic Press.

Yesavage, J. A. 1984. Relaxation and memory training in 39 elderly patients. *American Journal of Psychiatry* 141:778-81.

Yesavage, J. A., and T. L. Rose. 1984. Semantic elaboration and the method of loci: A new trip for old learners. *Experimental Aging Research* 10:155-60.

Yesavage, J. A., T. L. Rose, and G. H. Bower. 1983. Interactive imagery and affective judgments improve face-name learning in the elderly. *Journal of Gerontology* 38:197-203.

Zelinski, E. M., M. J. Gilewski, and L. W. Thompson. 1990. Do laboratory tests relate to self-assessment of memory ability in the young and old? In *New directions in memory and aging*, edited by L. W. Poon, J. L. Fozard, L. S. Cermak, D. Arenberg, and L. W. Thompson, 519-44. Hillsdale, NJ: Erlbaum.

Try these tools for remediating memory in your clients with head injuries . . .

FOCUS ON FUNCTION
Retraining for the Communicatively Impaired Client
by Shelly E. Hahn, M.A., CCC-SLP, and Evelyn Klein, Ph.D., CCC-SLP

Help your adolescent and adult clients improve functional communication with these practical, everyday activities. Activities are divided into these skill areas—verbal, phone, reading, writing, and numerical tasks. Reproducible worksheets and evaluations are included for therapy planning and use. **0761675515-YCS**

PROBLEM-SOLVING PICTURE CARDS
Daily Living Situations for Adults with Disabilities
by Mary John Pitti, M.S., CCC-SLP, and Traci Meier, M.S., CCC-SLP

Improve problem-solving and reasoning skills in your clients with brain injury! These 78 realistic full-color photographs show the unique problem situations clients face every day. The easy-to-use critical thinking questions on the reverse side of the photos prompt your clients to identify problems and determine and understand solutions. Concrete examples of everyday problem-solving situations cover Community Mobility, Confrontation, Safety, and more! **0761677984-YCS**

CONTEXTUAL MEMORY TEST
by Joan P. Toglia, M.A., OTR

Assess the awareness of memory capacity, strategy of memory use, and recall in your adult clients with memory dysfunction. Based on sound current theory, this standardized assessment is easy to use. You'll have extensive literature review, reliability data, scoring, and interpretation material. **0761647503-YTS**

BUILDING FUNCTIONAL SOCIAL SKILLS
Group Activities for Adults
by Angela Tipton Dikengil, M.S., CCC-SLP, and Monique Einbinder Kaye, M.S., CCC-SLP
Foreword by Dawn Stewart, OTR/L

Use this functional group model for adult clients who are neurologically impaired or who have traumatic brain injury. Develop important psycho-social skills necessary for effective interpersonal exchanges. Clients at Levels 5 to 8 on the *Rancho Los Amigos Levels of Cognitive Functioning* can begin with any of the units and progress according to your guidance. **0761642803-YTS**

COGNITIVE REHABILITATION
Group Games and Activities
by Joan P. Toglia, OTR, and Kathleen M. Golisz, OTR

This comprehensive resource features six specific group games designed for your adolescent and adult clients with brain injury. You'll have theoretical framework, game formats, descriptions and questions, and other group activities. Games cover the areas of Orientation, Long-Term Memory, Activities of Daily Living, Leisure, Financial, and Travel. A perfect resource for activity ideas as well as a guide to group treatment planning. **0761641955-YTS**

COGNITIVE-COMMUNICATION DISORDERS FOLLOWING TRAUMATIC BRAIN INJURY
A Practical Guide

by Jane Freund, B.Sc.(Log), S-LP(C), Carol Hayter, L.C.S.T., S-LP(C), Sheila MacDonald, M.Cl.Sc., S-LP(C), Mary Ann Neary, M.Sc.(A), S-LP(C), and Catherine Wiseman-Hakes, M.Sc., S-LP

Provide complete assessments and effective therapy for your clients of all ages with cognitive-communication disorders. A valuable reference, this program includes a theoretical framework and detailed information for treating clients with traumatic brain injury. Speech-language pathologists with TBI experience can expand their knowledge through detailed discussions of theory and current approaches to assessments and treatment.

0761630376-YCS

INTERACT
A Social Skills Game

by Holly Harper Love, M.A., OTR

Promote clients' learning of social skills with this interactive board game. Watch your clients become socially stimulated as they draw cards which elicit group discussions and role plays. The game is systematically structured so you can monitor progress. Use this game to develop skills for participation in society, to study the dynamics of small groups, and to promote positive changes in the group members.

0761640975-YTS

LANGUAGE ACTIVITY RESOURCE KIT (LARK)

by Richard A. Dressler, M.S., CCC-SLP

Here are the stimulus materials you need for adults who have language disorders! You'll have a portable kit based on 30 common objects that are familiar to adults—key, spoon, eyeglasses, and more. Each object is represented in these ways: two-sided illustrated cards, full-color photograph, word and phrase cards, and illustrated cards of each object in use. Designed specifically for itinerant clinicians with adult clients. Save time collecting the manipulatives for this kit—here are the basics ready for your use!

Complete kit, 0761673148-YCS
Cards and Manual only, 0761672613-YCS

COMMUNICATION CARRYOVER FOR ADULTS
Caregiver Information and Instruction

by Angela Tipton Dikengil, M.S., CCC-SLP

Send home information and instructions on a variety of speech and language topics, including dysphagia. Use these short, easy-to-understand handouts to provide daily carryover. Increase caregivers' understanding of communication problems experienced by adults.

0761671935-YCS

Address adult swallowing problems with these great products . . .

MANAGING DYSPHAGIA
An Instructional Guide for the Client and Family

by Brad Hutchins, M.A., CCC-SLP

Promote home carryover of dysphagia goals, treatment, and compensatory techniques with this video and informational workbooks. Motivate clients and families to participate fully in the rehabilitation process, while you save valuable explanation time! Using a single-family approach, total administration time takes only 30 minutes. **0761678034-YCS**

NUTRITIONAL MANAGEMENT OF DYSPHAGIA
A Therapist's Guide
by Pat Felt, M.S., RD, and Coleen Anderson, M.S., CCC-SLP

Address the nutritional needs of your adult clients with dysphagia. Help clients who are at risk for malnutrition by setting up a nutritional diet and educating client and caregiver. Refer to the manual for information on swallowing disorders, the properties of food, and the seven stages of the dysphagia diet. **0761647635-YTS**

SWALLOWING DISORDERS (Revised)
What Families Should Know
by Tom Rader, M.S., CCC-SLP, and Barbara Rende, M.S., CCC-SLP

These easy-to-follow booklets are useful resources for parents, families, and caregivers in home programming, workshops, and inservice training. Each booklet offers a case history, stages and symptoms of swallowing disorders, a glossary, and professional resources list. Sold in sets of 10. **076163004X-YCS**

For current prices on these practical resources, please call toll-free 1-800-228-0752.

ORDER FORM

Ship to:

Institution: _____

Name: _____

Occupation/Dept: _____

Address: _____

City: _____ State: _____ Zip: _____

Please check here if this is a permanent address change. ☐

Telephone No. _____ ☐ work ☐ home

Payment Options:

☐ Bill me.   ☐ My check is enclosed.

☐ My purchase order is enclosed. P.O. # _____

☐ Charge to my credit card: ☐ VISA ☐ MasterCard ☐ American Express

Card No. ☐☐☐☐☐☐☐☐☐☐☐☐☐☐☐☐

Expiration Date: Month _____ Year _____

Signature _____

Qty.	Cat. #	Title	Amount

Prices are in U.S. dollars. Payment must be made in U.S. funds only

- If your account is not currently listed as "tax exempt," applicable destination charges will be added to your invoice.
- Orders are shipped by United Parcel Service (UPS) unless otherwise requested. If another delivery service is required, please specify.
- For regular delivery service, your order will be charged 5% handling plus actual shipping charges.
- We occasionally backorder items temporarily out of stock. If you do not accept backorders, please tell us on your purchase order or on this form.

Money-Back Guarantee
You'll have up to 90 days of risk-free evaluation of the products your ordered. If you're not completely satisfied with any product, we'll pick it up within the 90 days and refund the full purchase price! **No questions asked!**

For Phone Orders
Call 1-800-228-0752. Please have your credit card and/or institutional purchase order information ready. Monday-Friday 7am-7pm Central Time. TDD 1-800-723-1318 / FAX 1-800-232-1223

Send your order to:
Communication Skill Builders
a division of The Psychological Corporation
555 Academic Court / San Antonio, Texas 78204-2498